THE PRESENT TESTAMENT
VOLUME FOUR
"FOOTSTEPS OF
THE GOOD SHEPHERD"
(THE LORD JESUS)

FOLLOW ME, KEN!

"MY INTERPRETATION OF THE HOLY BIBLE"

BARBARA ANN MARY MACK

THE PRESENT TESTAMENT VOLUME FOUR "FOOTSTEPS OF THE GOOD SHEPHERD" (THE LORD JESUS)

FOLLOW ME, KEN!

"MY INTERPRETATION OF THE HOLY BIBLE"

BARBARA ANN MARY MACK

authorHOUSE®

AuthorHouse™
1663 Liberty Drive
Bloomington, IN 47403
www.authorhouse.com
Phone: 1-800-839-8640

First published by AuthorHouse   07/01/2011

ISBN: 978-1-4634-1897-7 (sc)

TABLE OF CONTENTS

DEDICATION

TO JESUS, THE GOOD SHEPHERD AND KENNETH CHARLES BRABAZON JR.

ACKNOWLEDGMENT

MY LORD: YOUR GIFT OF LOVE FLOWS THROUGH THIS PIECE OF LITERARY GREATNESS, "YOUR HOLY ESSENCE".

I BLESS YOU; O HEAVENLY CREATOR AND GOD, FOR YOU HAVE SENT "YOUR GIFT OF LOVE" (GOD'S HOLY WORDS) TO YOUR LOVED ONES TODAY.

BARBARA ANN MARY MACK

INTRODUCTION

BARBARA SPEAKING TO THE HOLY TRINITY

MY LORD, YOU ARE "HOLY GROUNDS": YOUR GREAT CREATION ARE PRIVILEDGED TO WALK IN "YOUR HOLY PRECENCE" DAILY.

I AM YOURS, O "HOLY GROUNDS OF LOVE" (ALMIGHTY GOD): I AM "YOUR CHOSEN ONE" (BARBARA).

JOIN ME, O "HOLY GROUNDS", AS I BOW IN "YOUR HOLY PRESENCE", THROUGHOUT ETERNITY.

ALLELUIA! O LONGED FOR "HOLY SPOUSE" (THE HOLY TRINITY); ALLELUIA!!!

LIFT UP "YOUR CHOSEN BRIDE" (BARBARA), AS I APPROACH "YOUR HOLY GROUNDS OF LOVE".

LET ME FLY ON "YOUR HOLY WINGS OF LOVE" AS I TRAVEL THROUGH THIS WORLD OF EXISTENCE.

I AM "YOURS, O HOLY GROUNDS OF LOVE" (ALMIGHTY GOD); I AM "YOUR SOURCE OF CONTINUOUS DEVOTION AND COMMITMENT".

REACH FOR ME, O "HOLY GROUNDS" (ALMIGHTY GOD); REACH FOR "YOUR CHOSEN BRIDE" (BARBARA), THROUGHOUT ETERNITY!

ALLELUIA! O "HOLY SPOUSE (ALMIGHTY GOD) OF MINE"; ALLELUIA!!!

SING TO YOUR CHOSEN BRIDE (BARBARA), O "SWEET HOLY GROUNDS" (ALMIGHTY GOD), AS I CLING TO YOUR ETERNAL BEING THROUGHOUT THE DAY!

AS WE (BARBARA AND GOD'S OBEDIENT CHILDREN) BOW DOWN IN "THE PRESENCE OF HOLINESS" (ALMIGHTY GOD), WE WILL DEFEAT THE REALM OF EVIL AND DECEIT.

AS WE BOW DOWN IN "THE PRESENCE OF HOLINES" (ALMIGHTY GOD), WE WILL PRAISE "HIS HOLINESS" IN THE MIDST OF SATAN AND HIS SERVANTS OF SIN AND PAIN.

WE ARE YOURS, O "VICTORIOUS HOLY ONE" (ALMIGHTY GOD); WE ARE "YOUR SOLDIERS OF LOVE".

AS WE BOW DOWN TO "THE REALM OF HOLINESS" (ALMIGHTY GOD), WE WILL EXHIBIT "DIVINE LOVE" AMONG GOD'S CHILDREN OF ALL NAIONS AND RACES.

IN "YOUR HOLY PRESENCE, WE WILL SALUTE THE KING OF PEACE", MY LORD.

IN "YOUR HOLY PRESENCE" WE WILL GIVE YOU CONTINUOUS PRAISE, GLORY AND HONOR.

WE ADORE YOU, O "KING OF PEACE" (THE LORD JESUS).

WE REVERE YOU, O "SOVEREIGN ONE".

WE ARE YOURS, O RIGHTEOUS AND HOLY BROTHER (THE LORD JESUS) OF THE CHOSEN ONES.

WE ARE YOURS, O "FRIEND (THE LORD JESUS) OF THE FORGOTTEN ONES".

WE ARE YOURS, O "TUNNEL OF LOVE" (THE LORD JESUS).

WE ARE YOURS, O "ONLY BEGOTTEN SON OF OUR HOLY GROUNDS OF LOVE" (GOD, THE FATHER).

WE ARE YOURS, FOREVER! ALLELUIA! O "INVITING KING" (THE LORD JESUS); ALLELUIA!!!

AS WE BOW DOWN TO "HOLINESS" (ALMIGHTY GOD), WE WILL PRAISE YOU, LORD JESUS; IN "YOUR KINGDOM OF LOVE".

ALLELUIA!!! O "GREAT GOD" (THE LORD JESUS); ALLELUIA!!!

BARBARA SPEAKING TO GOD'S CREATION

GIVE HIM PRAISE, ALL WHO ARE CALLED TO WITNESS "HOLINESS" (ALMIGHTY GOD), THROUGHOUT ETERNITY!

GIVE "OUR LORD JESUS", CONTINUOUS PRAISE!!!

ALLELUIA!

THE LORD JESUS SPEAKING TO HIS CHILDREN

O BLESSED ONES; YOU HAVE BEEN CHOSEN TO WITNESS AND EXPERIENCE HOLINESS IN A WAY THAT NO OTHER HAS.

YOU HAVE BEEN CHOSEN TO "BREATHE THE AIR THAT PRODUCED THE GREAT CREATION THAT EXPRESSES DIVINE EXISTENCE".

REJOICE, O CHOSEN FLOCK OF LOVE, AS YOU WITNESS "THE GLORY THAT SURROUNDS THE GATES THAT LEAD TO HOLY GROUNDS" (ALMIGHTY GOD).

REJOICE, O CHOSEN ONES, IN "THE PRESENCE OF THE SAVING ONE" (THE LORD JESUS). FOR "HE REIGNS IN THE MIDST OF GLORY AND SPIRITUAL FAME"!

REJOICE, AS YOU WITNESS "THE SOUNDS OF LOVE THAT EMIT FROM HIS HOLY PRESENCE, DAILY".

REJOICE, AS YOU CAPTURE "THE ESSENCE OF THE HOLY GROUNDS OF LOVE" (ALMIGHTY GOD).

REJOICE, O CHOSEN FLOCK OF LOVE: REJOICE IN "THE PRESENCE OF HOLINESS" (ALMIGHTY GOD), THROUGHOUT ETERNITY.

LIFT UP YOUR WINGS AND FLY TO "THE REALM OF YOUR FIRST LOVE" (ALMIGHTY GOD), O CHOSEN ONES.

LIFT UP YOUR WINGS OF LOVE, AND FLY TO "YOUR SOURCE (THE LORD JESUS) OF CONTINUOUS LOVE AND PEACE".

LIFT UP YOUR WINGS AND FLY TO THE ENTRANCE OF, "THE REALM OF THE HOLY GROUNDS OF LOVE" (ALMIGHTY GOD).

ALLELUIA! O CHOSEN ONES; ALLELUIA!!!

BOOK ONE

"FOOT STEPS OF THE GOOD SHEPHERD"
(THE LORD JESUS)

SUBTITLE:

FOLLOW ME, KEN!

BY:

BARBARA ANN MARY MACK

DEDICATION

TO JESUS, THE GOOD SHEPHERD, AND KENNETH CHARLES BRABAZON JR.

ACKNOWLEDGMENT

MY LORD: YOUR GIFT OF LOVE HAS CAPTURED AND BLESSED YOUR CALLED AND CHOSEN SON, KENNETH CHARLES BRABAZON JR. YOUR LOVE FOR HIM IS EXPRESSED IN THE WRITINGS OF OUR (THE LORD AND BARBARA) **"ONE HUNDRED AND NINETIETH BBOK"**.

I BLESS YOU; O HEAVENLY CREATOR AND GOD, FOR YOU HAVE SENT "YOUR GIFT OF LOVE" (KEN) TO YOUR NEEDY SHEEP.

BARBARA ANN MARY MACK

PROLOGUE

<u>THE LORD JESUS SPEAKING TO THE SHEPHERDS OF HIS FLOCK ON</u>

<u>EARTH</u>

MY FOOTSTEPS WILL GUIDE YOU INTO "MY REALM ON HIGH" (HEAVEN).

FOLLOW ME, O PRECIOUS SHEPHERDS OF MY FLOCK ON EARTH, SO THAT I MAY LEAD YOU INTO A PASTURE THAT FLOWS WITH EVERLASTING MILK AND HONEY, WHICH IS "THE LEGACY OF MY LOVE AND HOLY PRESENCE".

FOLLOW ME INTO MY RIVERS OF CONTINUOUS SPIRITUAL NOURISHMENT, SO THAT YOU MAY BECOME FILLED WITTH "MY HOLY SPIRIT" AS YOU PREACH TO MY WANDERING FLOCK TODAY.

FOLLOW ME, O CHOSEN SHEPHERDS OF MY LITTLE ONES, SO THAT YOU MAY WITNESS PARADISE IN THE MIDST OF CONFUSION AND CHAOS.

FOLLOW "THE FOOTSTEPS OF THE GOOD SHEPHERD" (THE LORD JESUS), INTO "THE ARMS OF HEAVENLY BLISS" (ALMIGHTY GOD, THE FATHER)!

THE GIFT OF LOVE

GOD SPEAKING TO HIS CALLED AND CHOSEN SHEPHERDS

1.

YOUR ORDINATION INTO MY PRIESTLY CALL:

IS A "DIVINE EXPRESSION" THAT'S NOT GIVEN TO ALL.

2.

FOLLOW "THE FOOSTEPS OF MY LOVE":

SO THAT YOU WILL BE LED BY "MY HOLY DOVE".

3.

YOUR CALL IS HOLY AND CONTINUOUS, MY SON:

FOLLOW "THE VOICE OF THE ETERNAL ONE" (ALMIGHTY GOD).

4.

INTO THE LILLIES OF "MY FLOWING FIELD OF LOVE":

THAT IS "SANCTIFIED WITH THE PRESENCE OF MY HOLY DOVE" (SPIRIT)

5.

"THE GIFT OF LOVE" IS YOUR HOLY CALL:

TO PREACH TO: AND TEACH THOSE WHO WILL FALL.

6.

INTO THE PIT OF SIN, DESPAIR AND GLOOM,

THAT LEADS MY WANDERING SHEEP AWAY FOM "MY HOLY ROOM".

7.

"THE GIFT OF LOVE" HAS FOLLOWED YOU, MY SON;

INTO "THE ARMS OF THE HOLY ONE" (ALMIGHTY GOD).

I CAN SEE YOU, MY SON: MY CONDUIT

THE LORD SPEAKING TO KEN

1.

"MY HOLY PRESENCE" SURROUNDS MY CHOSEN SON (KEN) EVERYDAY:

I CAN SEE YOUR HEAVENLY GLOW, MY SON, AS YOU KNEEL TO PRAY.

2.

"YOUR HOLY PRESENCE IS GENUINE, PURE AND TRUE":

REJOICE! MY SON, FOR I HAVE CALLED AND CHOSEN YOU.

3.

REMAIN IN "MY HOLY WORDS" AS YOU LEAD MY FLOCK OF LOVE:

REMAIN IN "THE LIGHT OF MY HOLY DOVE" (SPIRIT).

4.

I CAN SEE YOU, MY SON, IN THE MIDST OF CHAOS AND FAME:

I CAN SEE YOU, MY SON, AS I CALL "YOUR HOLY NAME".

5.

REACH FOR "MY REALM OF PEACE AND TRANQUILITY", IN THE MIDST OF YOUR STORMY DAYS:

REACH FOR ME, DEAR SHEPHERD (KEN), AS YOU EXHIBIT "YOUR HOLY WAYS".

IN THE WINDS OF LOVE

<u>ALMIGHTY GOD SPEAKING TO KEN</u>

1.

IN "THE WINDS OF LOVE", I WILL CARRY YOU:

AS YOU DELIVER "MY MESSAGES" TO THE CHOSEN FEW.

2.

RIDE ON "THE WINDS OF LOVE", MY SON,

SO THAT YOU WILL REPRESENT "THE BATTLE THAT WE

(THE LORD AND KEN) HAVE WON".

3.

IN "THE WINDS OF LOVE, MY WORDS OF LIFE" WILL FLOW,

AS YOU SEARCH FOR "THE PRESENCE OF YOUR GOD'S

HOLY GLOW".

4.

I WILL TRAVEL WITH YOU, IN THE WINDS WITH 'MY HOLY DOVE":

AS YOU SHARE "YOUR HEAVENLY GIFTS WITH MY FLOCK OF LOVE".

5.

KENNETH, IN "THE WINDS OF LOVE" FLOWS YOUR GLOWING FACE,

AS YOU PROCLAIM "THE GOSPEL" TO THE HUMAN RACE.

6.

"THE WINDS OF LOVE" HAVE RELEASED "MY SACRED ESSENCE",
AS YOU PREACH "MY GOOD NEWS" IN THEIR WELCOMED PRESENCE.

CAN YOU FEEL "MY HOLY PRESENCE"?

<u>ALMIGHTY GOD SPEAKING TO HIS FLOCK</u>

1.

CAN YOU FEEL "MY HOLY PRESENCE"? O SEARCHING SHEEP OF MINE,

AS YOU LISTEN TO "MY VOICE", THROUGH MY MESSENGER (KEN) OF LOVE.

2.

I AM "IN THE MIDST", AS YOU SIT IN YOUR PEWS:

I WILL SPEAK THROUGH 'MY CHOSEN SHEPHERDS", AS THEY DELIVER "MY GOOD NEWS".

3.

"MY HOLY PRESENCE" IS TANGIBLE, WORTHY AND TRUE,

I AM NEAR, MY FLOCK: I AM SITTING NEXT TO YOU.

4.

CAN YOU FEEL "MY HOLY PRESENCE" THROUGHOUT THE DAY?

CAN YOU HEAR ME, DEAR CHILDREN, AS YOU KNEEL TO PRAY?

DELIVER "MY HOLY STORY"

ALMIGHTY GOD SPEAKING TO KEN

1.

TELL THEM ABOUT ME, O BLESSED SON (KEN) OF MINE,

SO THAT "MY HOLY STORY" WILL DWELL WITHIN THEM,

UNTIL THE END OF TIME.

2.

TELL THEM ABOUT "THE JOY THAT PERMEATES MY

HOLY LANDS":

TELL THEM OF "THE GOODNESS THAT'S RELEASED BY

MY HANDS".

3.

TELL THEM OF "MY GREATEST STORY" THAT FLOWS FROM "MY HOLY SCRIPTURES",
WHICH YOU PREACH OF:

TELL THEM, MY SON, ABOUT "MY ETERNAL LOVE".

4.

TELL THEM OF "THE JOY" THAT KNOWING ME OFFERS THE TRUSTING ONES:

TELL THEM ABOUT "THE PROTECTION" THAT SURROUNDS MY DAUGHTERS AND SONS.

5.

TELL THEM ABOUT "THE LOVE THAT FLOWS FROM THE BLESSED TRINITY":

TELL THEM, KEN, ABOUT YOU AND ME!

SMILE WITH ME, SAYS THE LORD

THE LORD SPEAKING TO KEN

1.

EXPRESS "THE LOVE THAT LIVES WITHIN YOUR CHOSEN

HEART",

AS YOU GREET MY LOVED ONES, AS THE NEW DAY

STARTS.

2.

SMILE WITH ME, O BLESSED SON (KEN) OF "THE

SACRED ONE" (ALMIGHTY GOD):

SHINE THROUGHOUT THE DAY, AS A WELL PLEASED

SON.

3.

"THE GIFTS OF JOY AND PEACE" HAVE CAPTURED

"YOUR RADIANT SMILE":

"THE GIFTS FROM ALMIGHTY GOD THAT HAVE

TRAVELED THROUGHOUT THE REALM OF TIME".

4.

"THE GIFT OF YOUR JOY" WILL ENLIGHTEN "MY FLOCK

OF LOVE",

AS YOU SHARE "THE MAGNIFICENCE OF YOUR HEAVENLY SMILE".

5.

SMILE THROUGHOUT THE DAY, AS YOU EXPRESS "YOUR

GIFT OF LOVE":

SMILE, MY SON, IN "THE PRESENCE OF YOUR GOD"!

I CAN SEE THE SUNSHINE

THE LORD SPEAKING TO KEN

1.

MY SON (KEN): I CAN SEE "THE SUNSHINE THAT EMITS

FROM YOUR GLOWING FACE":

SHARE "YOUR HEAVENLY RADIANCE WITH THE

BLESSED HUMAN RACE".

2.

"YOUR RADIANT GLOW IS SENT WITH GOD'S ETERNAL

HOLY SPIRIT":

SHINE ON MY FLOCK, DEAR SON, SO THAT ALL MAY SEE

IT!

3.

"YOUR RADIANT GLOW" LIGHTS UP THE DARKEST

NIGHT:

"YOUR RADIANT GLOW", DEAR SON, EXPRESSES "GOD'S

PHYSICAL MIGHT".

4.

RADIANCE PERMEATES "YOUR SACRED BEING":

COME, AND JOIN ME, MY SON, SO THAT WE MAY SING!

5.

SONGS OF "JOY, PRAISE, AND DELIGHT":

SONGS THAT EXPRESS "GOD'S HOLY MIGHT"!

YOU REPRESENT ME, THE GOOD SHEPHERD

THE LORD SPEAKING TO KEN

1.

YOU REPRESENT ME, O SON OF "MY HEAVENLY THRONE":

WALK WITH ME, O CHOSEN ONE (KEN), BECAUSE YOU ARE NEVER ALONE.

2.

BLOOM WITH "THE RADIANCE OF MY FLOWERS OF LOVE":

AS YOU PREACH TO MY FLOCK, "THE KNOWLEDGE OF MY HOLY DOVE" (SPIRIT).

3.

EXPRESS "MY ATTRIBUTES"; LOVE, JOY, AND PEACE:

EXPRESS "THE GOODNESS OF YOUR SHEPHERD (THE LORD JESUS) THAT MY THRONE HAS RELEASED".

4.

YOU REPRESENT "THE ATTRIBUTES OF JESUS, THE GOOD NEWS":

SPREAD "THE JOY OF MY HOLY PRESENCE TO THOSE WHO SIT IN MY PEWS".

5.

REPRESENT "YOUR GOD, AND FATHER OF LOVE":

REPRESENT "THE BLESSINGS" THAT ARE SENT FROM ABOVE.

6.

I LOVE TO SING AND DANCE WITH MY CHILDREN:

DELIVER "MY SONG", MY SON (KEN), TO EVERY NATION!

THE ROAD TO GLORY

THE LORD SPEAKING TO KEN

1.

APPROACH THE ROAD TO ETERNAL GLORY,

AS YOU DELIVER "MY HOLY STORY".

2.

TEACH THEM "MY WORDS OF ETERNAL SALVATION",

THAT ARE AVAILABLE TO ALL, FROM EVERY NATION.

3.

"THE ROAD TO ETERNAL GLORY" WILL LEAD YOU TO ME,

AS YOU SHARE "THE MESSAGES THAT COME FROM THE

HOLY TRINITY".

4.

"THE ROAD TO ETERNAL LIFE" MAY APPEAR LONG AND WEARY:

TO THOSE WHO REFUSE TO ACKNOWLEDGE AND WORSHIP ME.

5.

FREEDOM FROM PAIN AND SIN, WILL BE YOUR REWARD AS YOU SEEK ME:

COME, MY CHILDREN, AND FOLLOW "THE BLESSED TRINITY"!

6.

COME, MY SON (KEN), AND ENTER "MY GATE",

SO THAT YOU MAY ENJOY "THE GIFT OF YOUR FATE" (ETERNAL LIFE WITH THE HOLY TRINITY).

7.

A LIFE WITH ME, SO "GRAND AND PLENTY":

A LIFE THAT'S GOVERNED BY "THE HOLY TRINITY".

8.

YOUR (KEN) SHEEP WILL LISTEN TO "YOUR REALM OF

EXCITEMENT AND JOY",

AS YOU DANCE WITH ME, AS YOU DID WHEN YOU WERE A LITTLE BOY!

BOOK TWO

HAPPY BIRTHDAY, LA TOYA

LOVE, ALWAYS, MOMMY

BY:

BARBARA ANN MARY MACK

COMPOSED NOVEMBER 21, 2009

DEDICATION

TO LA TOYA ANN ROBINSON, A FAITHFUL SERVANT OF THE HOLY AND BLESSED TRINITY

ACKNOWLEDGMENT

MY HEAVENLY SOURCE (ALMIGHTY GOD) OF SPIRITUAL AND PHYSICAL NOURISHMENT: LA TOYA AND ME ACKNOWLEDGE "YOUR HOLY PRESENCE" IN HER LIFE. DEAR LORD: LA TOYA THRIVES FOR FAITHFULNESS AND OBEDIENCE UNTO HER CREATOR AND GOD DAILY. HER ALLEGIANCE UNTO "THE HOLY TRINITY AND HIS PRESENT DAY PROPHET" (BARBARA) CONVEYS BELIEF IN "THE CHRISTIAN FAITH".

I PRAISE YOU, DEAR LORD, FOR PLACING "THE GIFT OF LA TOYA", OUR DARLING DAUGHTER, IN MY LIFE.

BARBARA ANN MARY MACK

YOUR BIRTHDAY: A GIFT FROM ALMIGHTY GOD

GRACE (ALMIGHTY GOD) HAS OPENED "HIS SACRED ARMS", AND HAS RELEASED "THE GIFT OF HIS CHOSEN DAUGHTER" (LA TOYA) IN THE MIDST OF EARTH'S RESIDENTS.

GRACE (ALMIGHTY GOD) HAS OPENED "HIS HEAVENLY GATES, AND HAS RELEASED THE PRESENCE OF HIS CHOSEN DAUGHTER (LA TOYA), SO THAT SHE MAY SPREAD "THE GOODNESS OF HER GOD AND SAVIOR, THE LORD JESUS", WITH HER MOTHER (BARBARA ANN MARY MACK).

I AM NEAR, MY DARLING DAUGHTER (LA TOYA), I AM WITHIN "YOUR REALM OF TANGIBILITY".

THUS SAYS, THE LORD, YOUR GOD AND SAVIOR

A "BIRTHDAY GIFT" FOR YOU, FROM US (THE LORD AND BARBARA)

1.

HAPPY BIRTHDAY, DEAR LITTLE ONE (LA TOYA) WHO DWELLS WITHIN "MY GATES OF ETERNAL LOVE":

WE WILL CELEBRATE YOUR SPECIAL DAY, IN "THE PRESENCE OF GOD'S HOLY DOVE".

2.

A 'TOAST OF LOVE" WILL BEGIN YOUR SPECIAL DAY:

AS WE GIVE THANKS TO "YOUR ORIGIN" (ALMIGHTY GOD), AS WE KNEEL TO PRAY.

3.

PRAY, DEAR LITTLE ONE (LA TOYA), IN "THE PRESENCE OF HOLINESS" (ALMIGHTY GOD):

WE WILL PRAY, O SWEET BIRTHDAY GIRL, AS YOU GREET GOD'S INVITED GUESTS.

4.

TWENTY-SEVEN, TWENTY-SEVEN,

IS THE POWERFUL NUMBER THAT DESCENDED FROM HEAVEN.

5.

SHE (LA TOYA) ENTERED LIFE, IN "THE REALM OF TIME":

THAT RECEIVED "GOD'S GIFT" (LA TOYA), WITH OPENED ARMS.

6.

A "BREATH OF LOVE" (LA TOYA) FLOWED THROUGH "HEAVEN'S GATES":

AND ENTERED "LIFE'S REALM", WITH THE SMALL AND THE GREAT.

7.

YOU ARE FILLED WITH "LIFE'S ENERGY AND SPIRITUAL BLESSINGS":

CELEBRATE "YOUR SPECIAL DAY", AS YOU DANCE AND SING!

8.

SING TO THE MOUNTAINS, AND THE EVER-RUNNING HILLS:

DANCE, O BIRTHDAY GIRL, AS YOU ENJOY LIFE'S THRILLS!

9.

DANCE WITH YOUR FAMILY AND GRACEFUL FRIENDS:

DANCE, O SWEET BIRTHDAY GIRL, WITH "YOUR GOD, WHO REIGNS"!

10.

ANOTHER YEAR HAS GONE BY, AS YOU CELEBRATED IN THE STREETS OF JOY AND PEACE:

YOU HAVE CELEBRATED IN "THE PRESENCE OF THE LOVE (ALMIGHTY GOD) THAT WAS RELEASED"!

11.

EXPRESS "YOUR GRATITUDE" TO "YOUR LIFE SAVING GOD":

AS YOU DANCE THROUGHOUT ETERNITY, IN "THE PRESENCE OF DIVINE LOVE" (ALMIGHTY GOD)!

12.

ENJOY YOUR BIRTHDAY, AS THE END OF THE DAY APPROCHES:

ENJOY "YOUR DAY OF JOY WITH GOD'S ETERNAL HOLY GHOST" (SPIRIT)!

BOOK THREE

BATTLING SATAN, THE BEAST!

BY:

BARBARA ANN MARY MACK

COMPOSED APRIL 28, 2011 AROUND 10:00 P.M-APRIL 30, 2011 AROUND 9:40 P.M.

DEDICATION

TO LORD JESUS, THE DESTROYER OF EVIL (SATAN, THE BEAST)

ACKNOWLEDGMENT

MY LOVING LORD JESUS: O "ULTIMATE DESTROYER" OF EVERY EVIL WORK AND PERSONS: I HAVE UNITED WITH YOU IN THE BATTLE BEWEEN "GOOD" (ALMIGHTY GOD) AND EVIL (SATAN).

YOUR HOLY PRESENCE AND MIGHT ARE CONVEYED EMPHATICALLY WITHIN **"OUR ONE <u>HUNDRED AND EIGHTY-EIGHTH BOOK"</u>**.

I BLESS YOU CONTINUOUSLY, O GREAT AND HOLY ONE (THE LORD JESUS), FOR MAKING "YOUR MIGHT AND HOLY PRESENCE" KNOWN IN THE MIDST OF "THIS PERIOD OF GREAT TRIBULATION".

BARBARA ANN MARY MACK

PROLOGUE

ALMIGHTY GOD SPEAKING

HE (SATAN) ROAMS IN THE MIDST OF MY VULNERABLE CREATION, SPREADING DESTRUCTION AND DOOM WHERE EVER HE GOES!

HIS "UNHOLY PRESENCE" ECHOES THROUGH THE STREETS AND HOMES OF THE DOOMED ONES.

HE EXHIBITS NO MERCY, BECAUSE HAS NO KNOWLEDGE OF "MERCY"!

HE DOESN'T DISCRIMINATE, FOR HE IS THE DESTROYER!

HE HAS NO KNOWLEDGE OF LOVE, ONLY HATRED AND DESTRUCTION, FOR HE IS "SATAN, THE BEAST"!

HE IS "THE DESTROYER OF THE LIVING"!

HE IS "GARBAGE"!

HE IS "REJECTED" BY THOSE WHO KNOW AND FOLLOW "LORD JESUS, THE DESTROYER OF EVIL".

HE HAS BEEN CAST OUT OF HEAVEN BY ALMIGHTY GOD, BECAUSE OF HIS EVIL THOUGHTS AND PLANS.

HE IS DOOMED! HE IS LIFELESS! HE WILL PAY FOR HIS CRIMES AGAINST HUMAN BEINGS.

HIS TIME IS COMING TO A "GLORIOUS CONCLUSION", FOR LORD JESUS, "THE DESTROYER OF EVIL", HAS TAKEN THE STAND, IN THE MIDST OF EARTH'S INHABITANTS TODAY!

LET "VICTORY" RING THROUGHOUT THE TRIUMPHANT STREETS AGAIN!!! ALLELUIA!!!

HIS (SATAN) UNHOLY PRESENCE

BARBARA SPEAKING

HIS (SATAN) PRESENCE IS "UNWANTED"!
HIS UNHOLY PRESENCE IS NOT WELCOMED!

BARBARA SPEAKING TO SATAN

REMOVE YOURSELF; O DESTRUCTIVE ONE (SATAN), FOR LORD JESUS, THE DESTROYER, IS ON YOUR TAIL TODAY!

THE LORD JESUS IS ON YOUR TRAIL OF DESTRUCTION, FOR YOU HAVE CAUSED GREAT AND CONTINUOUS DESTRUCTION IN HIS HOLY SIGHT TODAY.

BARBARA SPEAKING TO GOD'S CHILDREN

HE (THE LORD JESUS) HAS RETURNED, TO GIVE PEACE AND COMFORT TO THOSE WHO FOLLOW AND TRUST HIM, IN THE MIDST OF THIS TERRIBLE PERIOD IN HISTORY.

RELY ON THE POWER AND MIGHT OF LORD JESUS, FOR HE IS GREATER THAN SATAN, THE BEAST.

HE (THE LORD JESUS) IS GREATER THAN DESTRUCTION.
HE IS GREATER THAN "DOOM"!
HE IS "THE SAVIOR" IN THE MIDST OF TRIBULATIONS AND STORMS.

HE IS "THE RESCUER OF SINKING DOOMED SOULS".
HE IS "THE REVIVER" AND "SURVIVOR"!

HE IS "ALMIGHTY GOD"!

HE IS ALPHA (THE BEGINNING, AND THE FIRST)!
HE IS "HOLY PRESENCE IN OUR MIDST"!
HE IS LORD OF LORDS!

HE IS "KING JESUS"!!!
HE IS "THE GREAT REVIVER"!
HE IS "THE DEDICATED ONE"!
HE IS THE ENTRANCE TO LIFE!!!

BARBARA SPEAKING TO SATAN

I SEE YOUR (SATAN) UNHOLY PRESENCE IN THE NUMEROUS STORMS THAT HAVE TAKEN THE LIVES OF MANY VULNERABLE SOULS.

I SEE YOUR UNHOLY PRESENCE IN THE CRIMES THAT FLOW IN THE MIDST OF EVERY NATION.

I SEE YOUR UNHOLY PRESENCE IN THE LACK OF LOVE AND UNITY THAT ARE VISIBLE AMONG GOD'S CHILDREN.

I SEE YOU, O DESTROYER (SATAN) OF LIFE: I SEE YOU IN THE MIDST OF PAIN AND DESTRUCTION.

WE (THE LORD AND BARBARA) WILL REMOVE YOU FROM THE LIVES OF THE INNOCENT ONES.

WE WILL REMOVE YOU FROM THE LIVES OF THOSE WHO BELIEVE IN ALMIGHTY GOD'S MIGHT OVER SATAN'S.

WE WILL REMOVE YOU, O REALM OF HARM (SATAN, THE BEAST): WE WILL REMOVE YOUR DESTRUCTION SOON!

SO, PREPARE YOURSELF FOR YOUR DESTINATION IN HELL, FOR IT IS YOUR DESTINTY! IT IS YOUR PERMANENT RESIDENCE!

IT IS YOUR FUTURE!
IT IS YOUR PAST!
IT IS YOUR PRESENT!

BEHOLD, O REALM OF DESTRUCTION (SATAN): YOU ARE DOOMED!!!

YOUR UNHOLY PRESENCE HAS CAUSED CONTINUOUS DESTRUCTION FOR THOUSANDS OF YEARS:

WE WILL NO LONGER TOLERATE YOUR ABUSE TOWARDS GOD'S CHILDREN.

THERE IS NO PLEADING WITH YOU, O REALM OF DESTRUCTION (SATAN, THE BEAST):

THERE IS NO REASONING WITH YOU, FOR YOU ARE THE EPITOME OF DOOM AND DEATH.

YOU ARE DARKNESS; YOU ARE PAIN: YOU ARE DESTRUCTION IN THE MIDST OF CHAOS!

PLEADING WITH YOU HAS NO GAIN.

YOU LAUGH AT THOSE WHO PLEAD TO YOU FOR RELIEF.
YOU HINDER THE PRODUCTION OF MY HOLY WORK.
YOU, O SATAN, IS AN "UNWANTED BUM"!

YOU HAVE INFLICTED ME WITH PHYSICAL AILMENTS, TO PREVENT OR HINDER MY WORK FOR THE LORD.

YOU HAVE TAMPERED WITH THE PRODUCTION OF MY BOOKS.

YOU PREVENT THE RECEPTION OF MY EMAIL MESSAGE TO MY BELOVED ONE (CRAIG) AND OTHER RECIPIENTS OF GOD'S HOLY MESSAGES:

YOU, O SATAN, ARE AN "UNWANTED BUM"!

YOUR "UNHOLY PRESENCE MAKES ME SICK".

KNOWLEDGE OF YOUR UNHOLY PRESENCE CAUSES ME TO ATTACK YOU MORE, BY SHARING "THE GOOD NEWS OF ALMIGHTY GOD'S PRESENCE IN OUR MIDST TODAY"!

I CANNOT STAND YOUR UNHOLY PRESENCE!
I TRULY HATE YOU, O LIFELESS ONE (SATAN)!
FOR, YOU TRY TO DESTROY "GOD'S GOOD AND HOLY WORKS", DAILY).

YOU WHO CRAWL FROM THE PIT OF STENCH DAILY, I HATE EVERYTHING ABOUT YOU AND YOUR WORLD OF DECEPTION AND DEFEAT, FOR, "DIVINE LOVE AND MERCY PERMEATE MY OBEDIENT SOUL DAILY".

YOU TRY DESPARATELY TO TURN ALL GOOD CHRISTIANS AWAY FROM "GOD'S HOLY WAY".

WE (BARBARA AND GOD'S FAITHFUL CHILDREN) DO NOT LIKE YOU, O EVIL PRESENCE THAT SLITHERS THROUGH EARTH'S RESIDENTS HOMES, PLAY AND WORK PLACES.

YOUR FOLLOWERS WILL ROT IN THE PIT OF DESTRUCTION (HELL) WITH YOU, AT THE APPOINTED TIME".

OH WHAT "A DAY OF ANTICIPATED JOY"!

MY TIME OF REJOICING! MY TIME OF CELEBRATION! MY TIME OF CONTINUOUS LAUGHTER! MY TIME OF PEACE!

THOSE WHO ROB AND STEAL WILL JOIN YOUR REALM OF ETERNAL DOOM!

THOSE WHO MURDER AND ABUSE GOD'S CREATION WILL SHARE THE PIT OF HELL WITH YOU (SATAN).

YOUR DAY OF END IS APPROACH: BEWARE!!!

BARBARA SPEAKS TO THE FOLLOWERS OF EVIL (SATAN)

BE AWARE OF YOUR DESTINATION IN HELL, ALL WHO GAMBLE AND ABUSE ALCOHOLIC BEVERAGES, FOR YOU PERFORM THE BEHAVIOR OF AN UNHOLY ONE, IN THE PRESENCE OF THE LORD.

BE AWARE OF YOUR DESTINATION IN HELL, ALL THAT COMMIT SUICIDE (MURDER), FOR YOU HAVE TAKEN THE LIFE OF A CHILD OF MINE, AND I AM DISPLEASED.

BARBARA SPEAKING TO THE LORD

MY LORD: SOME OF THE MEDICATIONS THAT ARE PRESCRIBED TO YOUR LOVED ONES HAVE CAUSED THEM TO COMMIT SUICIDE: ARE THEY PARDONED? DEAR LORD.

I HAVE BEEN GIVEN PRESCRIBED MEDICATION THAT STATED SUICIDE THOUGHTS AND ACTIONS AS SIDE EFFECTS: WITH THAT KNOWLEDGE, I DID NOT TAKE THE MEDICATION, THEREFORE, I CHOSE NOT TO PLACE MYSELF IN THE POSITION OF POSSIBLE SUICIDE THOUGHTS OR ACTIONS.

WE DO HAVE A CHOICE BEFORE TAKING THE MEDICATION.

WE DO NOT HAVE TO DESTROY OURSELVES. SATAN PLACES SUICIDAL THOUGHTS IN THE MINDS OF THE WEAK AND DEPRESSED ONES.

SUICIDE IS THE ULTIMATE DESTRUCTION TO ONE'S PHYSICAL BEING AND ETERNAL SOUL.

SUICIDE GIVES THE RECIPIENT ACCESS TO SPENDING ETERNITY WITH THE REALM OF DESTRUCTION: ONE DESTROYS GOD'S CREATION (HUMAN BEING) WHEN HE OR SHE COMMITS SUICIDE (MURDER).

SPIRITUAL, EMOTIONAL AND PHYSICAL PAIN CAUSE ONE TO ACT OUT SUICIDAL BEHAVIOR.

THE PAIN IS TREMENDOUS, AND VERY HEAVY; TOO MUCH FOR ONE TO CARRY ALONE.

WITH THE KNOWLEDGE AND STRENGTH OF ALMIGHTY GOD, AND A GOOD FRIEND THAT WILL LISTEN TO THE DESPAIRED ONE: WILL PREVENT SUICIDAL THOUGHTS AND ACTIONS.

SATAN PREYS ON THE DESPAIRED ONES.

HE LURES THE HOPELESS ONES INTO HIS REALM OF DOOM, WHICH ULTIMATELY ENDS IN DEATH.

HE IS A DECEIVER OF THE HOPELESS ONES: HE IS A DECEIVER OF THE FRIENDLESS ONES.

HE INVITES THE LONELY ONES INTO HIS WEB OF DECEIT AND TEMPORARY RELIEF AND JOY.

FOR HE IS THE ULTIMATE DECEIVER: THE DOOMED ONE! DEATH!

SPIRITUAL DARKNESS AND PAIN. LIFELESS! A PERMANENT RESIDENT OF HELL!

BARBARA SPEAKING TO SATAN, THE BEAST

WHERE WILL YOU RUN TO, WHEN THE APPOINTED TIME OF YOUR DEPARTURE FROM EARTH ARRIVES?

WHO WILL YOU TURN TO FOR RELIEF FROM THE FIRES OF HELL?

THERE IS NO ESCAPE FOR YOU, O LIFELESS ONE (SATAN)!

THERE IS NO ESCAPE FOR YOU, O PRINCE (SATAN) OF DOOM!

THERE IS NO ESCAPE FOR YOU (SATAN), O WELL OF PAIN AND TORTURE!

THERE IS NO ESCAPE FOR THE ETERNAL RESIDENTS (SATAN AND HIS FOLLOWERS, THOSE WHO COMMIT SIN) OF HELL!!!

BUT, THERE IS "HOPE" FOR THOSE WHO ESCAPE YOUR (SATAN) REALM OF DOOM.

THERE IS "HOPE" FOR THOSE WHO ACKNOWLEDGE AND LIVE A HOLY LIFE.

THERE IS "HOPE" FOR THOSE WHO FOLLOW "THE TEACHINGS AND WORDS OF THE ONLY SAVIOR" (THE LORD JESUS).

THERE IS "HOPE" FOR THE BELIEVERS.

THE LORD JESUS SPEAKING TO HIS CHILDREN

"COME TO ME, SAYS THE SAVIOR, CHRIST JESUS, FOR THERE IS HOPE IN ME, ALONE!"

THERE IS LIFE IN ME!
THERE IS SPIRITUAL GAIN IN ME!
THERE IS PHYSICAL GAIN IN ME!

"COME TO ME!" ALL WHO BELIEVE.

THE REALM (ALMIGHTY GOD) THAT BATTLES SATAN, THE BEAST DAILY

BARBARA SPEAKING TO SATAN, THE BEAST

"THE REALM OF VICTORY" (ALMIGHTY GOD) WILL WIPE YOU OFF OF THE FACE OF THE EARTH VERY SOON; O DOOMED ONE (SATAN)!

"THE REALM OF VICTORY" HAS CLAIMED YOUR UNWANTED EXISTENCE, O FOUL ONE (SATAN, THE BEAST)!

"THE REALM OF VICTORY" HAS PLACED YOUR UNWANTED FOUL PRESENCE IN "THE REALM OF APPOINTED TIME", SO THAT YOU WILL ENTER YOUR DESTINATION ON TIME (SOON).

YOU PROWL BY DAY, AND BY NIGHT, SNATCHING THE SOULS THAT ARE NOT WITHIN "THE REALM OF HOLINESS" (ALMIGHTY GOD).

YOU ENTER THE HOMES AND WORK PLACES OF THOSE WHO REJECT "THE REALITY OF DIVINE CREATION".

YOU INVADE THE PLACES OF ENTERTAINMENT, WHICH LURE THOSE WHO DO NOT KNOW ME, FREQUENTLY, SAYS THE LORD.

YOU NO LONGER HIDE IN THE SHADOWS, OR PRESENT YOUR PRESENCE IN AN INCONSPICUOUS MANNER, FOR THOSE WHO DO NOT FOLLOW THE LORD, ARE EAGER TO DWELL IN THE MIDST OF YOUR PRETENSE OF GOOD THINGS AND TIMES.

YOU NO LONGER FEEL THE NEED TO LURE THE VULNERABLE ONES INTO YOUR REALM OF UNHOLINES, FOR THEY ARE AWARE OF YOUR WORKS AND DESTINATION: BUT DO THEY REALLY BELIEVE OR UNDERSTAND THE SEVERITY OF IT?

BARBARA SPEAKING TO THOSE WHO ARE WALKING IN SATAN'S FOOTSTEPS

WAKE UP! ALL WHO DO NOT KNOW OR UNDERSTAND THE TRUTH ABOUT HELL AND SATAN, THE BEAST,

WAKE UP! ALL WHO DO NOT WANT TO SPEND ETERNITY (FOREVER) IN A PLACE OF CONTINUOUS PAIN AND MISERY.

WAKE UP! YOU WHO ROAM WITH SATAN AND HIS REALM OF TORTURE, FOR THE DAY OF THE LORD'S VENGEANCE DRAWS NEAR, AND YOU WILL NOT ESCAPE HIS PUNISHMENT.

WAKE UP! O FOLLOWERS OF DARKNESS AND DESTRUCTION (SATAN): FOR "THE WRATH OF THE LORD" IS KNOCKING ON YOUR DOORS.

AND YOU WILL NOT ESCAPE HIS MIGHTY HAND!

WAKE UP, O SLEEPING ONES, FOR "THE DAY OF THE LORD" IS APPROACHING YOU!

YOU HAVE INFLICTED EVIL ACTS ON THE MEEK AND VULNERABLE ONES.

YOU SHOW KNOW MERCY OR REMORSE FOR YOUR EVIL ACTS.

THE TABLES WILL TURN SOON, O EVIL ONES: YOUR DAY OF VULNERABILITY IS APPROACHING!

YOUR DAY OF PAIN AND SUFFERING WILL COME (VERY SOON):

THOSE WHOM YOU HAVE TORTURED WILL WITNESS YOUR SUFFERING AND PAIN.

THOSE WHOM YOU SHOWED NO MERCY, WILL WITNESS THE WRATH THAT COMES WITH OUR "VICTORIOUS KING JESUS", AS HE LASHES OUT AT THOSE WHO HAVE HARMED HIS CHILDREN OVER THE CENTURIES.

BEHOLD, O WORKERS OF EVIL, FOR "THE CLOCK IS TICKING": THE TIME IS APPROACHING! YOUR DAY OF DESTRUCTION BOWS IN FRONT OF YOU EACH DAY, FOR IT IS "THE APPOINTED TIME"!!!

DOOM HAS OPENED THE GATES TO HELL! ENTER, FOR YOUR DESTINATION AWAITS YOU TODAY!!!

SATAN, THE REALM OF
CRUELTY AND PAIN

<u>BARBARA SPEAKING TO SATAN AND HIS FOLLOWERS</u>

YOU HAVE MADE MANY LITTLE BABIES SUFFER!
YOU HAVE INFLICTED PAIN ON THE VULNERABLE CHILDREN.
YOU HAVE CAUSED THEIR DEATHS IN A HORRIBLE MANNER.
YOU HAVE TORTURED AND KILLED INNOCENT MOTHERS.
YOU HAVE MURDERED THE NEEDED HUSBANDS AND FATHERS.
YOU HAVE SHOWED NO MERCY: YOU SHOWED NO REMORSE.

LET THE CURTAINS DESCEND, FOR YOUR PUNISHMENT AWAITS YOU, O DOOMED
ONES.

PREPARE TO MEET "THE GREAT AND HOLY JUDGE" (ALMIGHTY GOD), FOR HE IS
WITHIN YOUR UNHOLY PRESENCE TODAY!

YOU ARE SO CRUEL, O EVIL ONE (SATAN): YOU ARE THE EPITOME OF CONTINUOUS
CRUELTY AND TORTURE.

YOU WILL ROT IN HELL, O INITIATOR OF ONGOING PAIN AND SUFFERING.

YOU SIR, ARE AN UNWANTED BUM!

YOUR ACTS OF CRUELTY AND INFLICTED PAIN HAVE NOT HINDERED MY WORK FOR
THE LORD.

YOUR ACTS OF CRUELTY AND INFLICTED PAIN HAVE NOT CAUSED MY BELOVED
(CRAIG) AND ME TO ABANDON EACH OTHER.

YOU TRY DAILY TO DESTROY A LOVE THAT DESCENDED WITH GOD'S APPROVAL
AND BLESSINGS, O DEFEATED ONE (SATAN).

YOU TRY DAILY TO TERMINATE A LOVE THAT IS EVER LASTING.

YOU TRY DAILY TO DESTROY A LOVE, WHICH CANNOT BE DESTROYED.

REMOVE YOURSELF FROM OUR REALM OF HAPPINESS, FOR YOUR PRESENCE AND STENCH ARE NOT WANTED!!!

MY BELOVED (CRAIG, THE LORD AND BARBARA'S PRAYER WARRIOR) AND I WILL CONTINUE FIGHTING YOU WITH "THE GIFT OF OUR SINCERE LOVE FOR ALMIGHTY GOD AND EACH OTHER".

WE HAVE TAKEN MANY RISKS FOR "OUR DIVINE LOVE".

WE HAVE MADE "MANY SACRIFICES FOR THE SAKE OF OUR HEAVEN SENT UNION".

YOU, O LOWLY ONE (SATAN), ARE A BUM!

YOUR ACTS OF CRUELTY TOWARD ALL OF GOD'S CHILDREN, HAVE CAUSED MY HATE FOR YOU TO GROW; AND INCREASED MY EXPRESSIONS OF LOVE FOR MY BELOVED ONE AND THOSE WHO HAVE OFFENDED US.

GET BENEATH THE DIRT WHERE YOU WILL RESIDE SOON, O UNWANTED RING OF FILTH (SATAN)!

ENTER THE UNDER WORLD OF DARKNESS AND DEATH, O RING OF THIEVES (SATAN AND HIS SERVANTS OF EVIL)!

ENTER YOUR REALM OF DOOM TODAY! FOR, DARKNESS AND ETERNAL DEATH AWAITS YOU!!!

YOU WILL EXPERIENCE GREAT SUFFERING, O PRINCE (SATAN) OF DOOM!

YOU WILL EXPERIENCE THE TOTAL LEVEL OF SUFFERING THAT YOU EMITTED OVER THE CENTURIES!

YOU WILL PAY FOR ALL OF THE MISERY THAT YOU HAVE INFLICTED ON GOD'S GREAT CREATION (HUMAN BEINGS).

ALMIGHTY GOD SPEAKING TO SATAN

YOU HAVE SENT YOUR SERVANTS OF LIES AND DECEIT TO MY VULNERABLE CHILDREN, SO THAT THEY WOULD BETRAY AND DEPART FROM MY REALM OF TRUTH.

YOU WILL PAY HEAVILY FOR YOUR ACTS OF CRUELTY.

FOR I AM VENGEANCE!!!

I AM YOUR ANNIHILATOR, O SATAN!
I AM YOUR DESTROYER!!!
I AM ALMIGHTY GOD!!!

YOU ENTER THE LIFELESS BODIES OF THOSE WHO WALK IN DARKNESS.

YOU ENTER THE BODIES OF THOSE WHO ENTER THE CHURCH BUILDINGS, WITHOUT REVERENCE OR ACKNOWLEDGMENT OF THEIR HOLY GOD AND CREATOR.

YOU GAIN ACCESS TO THE SHEPHERDS OF THE WORLD'S CHURCHES, BECAUSE THEY DO NOT KNOW ME.

YOU HAVE NO PROBLEM ENTERING THE BEINGS OF THE WORLD'S CLERGY, BECAUSE THEY SEEK THE PRAISE OF THE WORLD, INSTEAD OF PRAISING THEIR CREATOR AND GOD.

YOU CAN HAVE THEM, O PRINCE (SATAN) OF DOOM, FOR THEY ARE YOUR SERVANTS.

THEY ARE YOUR REWARD: THEY ARE PRODUCTS OF YOUR UNHOLY PRESENCE TODAY.

THEY TOO, ARE DOOMED!!!

I HAVE WITNESSED THEIR UNHOLY ACTS THROUGH THE YEARS: I HAVE WITNESSED THEIR MERCILESS DEEDS.

THEY WILL FEEL THE ENDLESS FIRE! FOR THEY ARE DOOMED!

THEY ARE THE INHABITANTS OF HELL! THEY ARE THE RESIDENTS OF THE ABYSS!

THEY ARE THE PRODUCTS OF EVIL. THEY ARE SATAN, THE BEAST'S SERVANTS. THEY ARE DOOMED!!!

THOSE WHO GET PLEASURE FROM INFLICTING PAIN ON MY CHILDREN: YOU ARE DAMNED!!!

THOSE WHO CURSE ME IN MY HOLY PRESENCE: YOU ARE DAMNED!!!

THOSE WHO HAVE ABUSED AND DISRESPECTED MY HOLY QUEEN (BARBARA): YOU ARE DAMNED!!!

THOSE WHO PLACE THE WORLD OVER MY HEAVENLY AND EARTHLY KINGDOMS: YOU ARE DAMNED!!!

THOSE WHO DISHONOR "THE SABBATH DAY": YOU ARE DAMNED!!!

COME, O DAMNED ONES, AND ENTER "YOUR FINAL TOMB" (HELL): FOR YOU HAVE CHOSEN TO DWELL IN "THE PIT THAT EMITS CONTINUOUS FIRE AND DESTRUCTION"!!!

YOU HAVE CHOSEN YOUR PERMANENT PLACE OF EXISTENCE.

THERE WILL BE NO PEACE FOR YOU IN THE ABYSS.

THERE WILL BE NO JOY FOR YOU IN HELL.

THERE WILL BE NO PERIODS OF LAUGHTER AND GLEE, FOR YOU HAVE ENTERED THE RESIDENCE OF THE DAMNED!!!

YOU MAY WEEP, BUT YOUR CRIES WILL NOT BE HEARD!

YOU MAY BEG, BUT YOUR PLEAS WILL NOT BE HEARD!

YOU MAY SHOUT WITH GRIEF, BUT YOUR SOUNDS WILL NOT GET A HELPFUL RESPONSE.

FOR YOU HAVE BEEN SENTENCED TO ETERNAL DAMNATION!

THE GREAT AND MIGHTY JUDGE (GOD) HAS PERFORMED "HIS FINAL TASK WITH THE REALM OF EVIL" (SATAN).

EARTH WILL FINALLY REJOICE IN THE PRESENCE OF FREEDOM (ALMIGHTY GOD), FOR SATAN, THE BEAST, HAS BEEN CONSUMED IN HELL!

LET THE ENTRANCE TO HELL SHUT FOREVER, FOR ITS RESIDENTS (SATAN AND HIS SERVANTS) HAS ENTERED!!!

EPILOGUE

THE HOLY SPIRIT SPEAKING

THE BATTLE HAS ENDED! THE WAR IS OVER! THE VICTORIOUS ONES (ALMIGHTY GOD, BARBARA, FR. CRAIG DE PAULO; THE BELOVED ONE, LA TOYA, AMYA PENNY AND GOD'S HOST OF OBEDIENT CHILDREN) HAVE MADE KNOWN OF "THEIR VICTORY" OVER SATAN, THE BEAST.

HEAVEN AND EARTH WITNESS SATAN'S ENTRANCE INTO THE ABYSS.

HELL'S DOORS HAVE CLOSED, FOR ITS "PERMANENT RESIDENTS" (SATAN AND HIS FOLLOWERS) ARE FINALLY HOME (HELL)!

"COMPLETION AND VICTORY BOW IN THE PRESENCE OF THE VICTORIOUS KING" (THE LORD JESUS), FOR HE HAS DEFEATED SATAN, THE BEAST, IN "THE PRESENCE OF GOD, THE FATHER"!

ALLELUIA!!!

BOOK FOUR

THE JOY OF THE LORD

SUBTITLE:

WHAT I ORDAINED

BY:

BARBARA ANN MARY MACK

COMPOSE MAY 1, 2011 AT 3:15 P.M.-MAY 1, 2011 11:56 P.M.

FATHER KENNETH CHARLES BRABAZON, JR. ORDAINED INTO THE ROMAN CATHOLIC CHURCH, MAY 21, 2011. CONGRATULATIONS FATHER KEN

DEDICATION

TO FULFILLMENT (ALMIGHTY GOD) AND FATHER KENNETH CHARLES BRABAZON, JR.

ACKNOWLEDGMENT

I ACKNOWLEDGE YOUR WORDS AS BEING TRUTH AND HOLY, DEAR LORD: WHAT YOU REVEAL COMES TO PASS!

YOUR WORDS ARE HOLY AND ENLIGHTENING: YOUR WORDS PERMEATE **"MY ONE HUNDRED AND EIGHTIETY-NINETH BOOK"**

I BOW CONTINUOUSLY IN THE PRESENCE OF YOUR HOLY WORDS, DAILY, DEAR LORD!

BARBARA ANN MARY MACK

PROLOGUE

WHAT I SAY WILL COME INTO EXISTENCE, BECAUSE I AM NOT A GOD WHO LIES OR MISLEAD MY CHILDREN.

MY WORDS HELP MY CHILDREN COME CLOSER TO MY WELL OF TRUTH: THEREFORE, I WILL CONTINUE SENDING THEM FULFILLED PROMISES.

EVERYTHING THAT I ORDAIN AS THRUTH COMES INTO EXISTENCE, SO THAT MY CHILDREN WILL FILL THE JOY OF THEIR GREAT AND HOLY GOD: FOR I CARE A GREAT DEAL FOR MY LITTLE CHILDREN OF ALL AGES, RACES AND NATIONS.

MY HOLY WORD HAS CARRIED MY CHILDREN THROUGH THE YEARS: AND THEY WILL CONTINUE LEADING THEM CLOSER TO MY REALM OF HOLY JOY.

THOSE WHO KNOW AND TRUST ME REVERE MY WORDS AND PROMISES, FOR THEY ARE HOLY. THEY ARE LIFE: THEY ARE LIGHT:

THEY ARE SALVATION: THEY ARE PEACE: THERY ARE REVIVAL:

THEY ARE LIVING WATER: THEY ARE HOPE: THEY ARE EVERLASTING.

THEY ARE MY PROMISE TO MANKIND.

THUS SAYS, THE LORD

MY WORD, MY PROMISE

<u>THE HOLY ONE (ALMIGHTY GOD) SPEAKS TO HIS CHILDREN OF</u>

<u>EVERY NATION</u>

WALK WITH MY HOLY WORDS, DEAR CHILDREN, SO THAT YOU MAY DWELL WITHIN THE GATES OF JOY EVERY DAY.

WALK WITH MY HOLY WORDS EACH DAY, SO THAT I MAY SHARE MY LOVE WITH YOU.

WALK WITH MY HOLY WORDS, SO THAT YOU MAY GAIN KNOWLEDGE OF YOUR DESTINATION: FOR MY WORDS REVEAL THE SECRET TO FUTURE OCCURRENCES.

MY WORDS REVEAL MY PLANS FOR YOUR LIFE ON EARTH, AND IN HEAVEN (ETERNAL GLORY).

WALK WITH MY HOLY WORDS, FOR THEY SPEAK MY TRUTH.

I WILL TELL YOU HOW TO LIVE A LIFE THAT'S FREE OF ANXIETY AND PAIN.

I WILL TELL YOU HOW TO TRUST IN ME, ALONE: FOR I WILL NEVER FORSAKE YOU OR LEAVE YOU IN THE STREETS OF DESPAIR.

I WILL NEVER LEAVE YOU ALONE WHEN HARM KNOCKS ON YOUR DOORS.

DESPITE WHAT IT APPEARS: I AM ALWAYS IN YOUR MIDST, BECAUSE YOU ARE MY GREATEST CREATION; MY JOY!

WALK WITH MY HOLY WORDS, MY CHILDREN, AS YOU APPROACH EACH DAY, AND I WILL HELP YOU DEAL WITH THE TRAGEDIES THAT WILL OCCU IN YOUR LIFE.

I WILL STAND BY YOU WHEN YOU ARE LOST FOR WORDS OF COMFORT TO YOUR FRIENDS AND NEIGHBORS, WHEN TRAGEDY SURROUNDS THEM.

I WILL HELP YOU WHEN YOUR CUPBOARDS AND EMPTY, AND WHEN YOU HAVE NO PLACE TO REST WHEN YOU GROW WEARY.

MY WORDS WILL HELP YOU CALL OUT TO ME, BECAUSE I ALONE CAN RELIEVE YOU FROM YOUR PROBLEMS AND PAIN.

I, ALONE, KNOW EVERYTHING THAT GOES ON BEFORE AND AFTER ITS OCCURRENCE.

AND I, ALONE, CAN RELIEVE MY CHILDREN FROM HARM, FOR I AM ALMIGHTY GOD.

I AM THE OMNIPRESENT ONE!

I AM YOUR ETERNAL SOURCE OF CONTINUOUS HELP.

I AM YOUR CREATOR AND HEAVENLY FATHER.

COME TO MY HOLY WORDS, DEAR CHILDREN, FOR THEY ARE CALLING YOU TODAY!

COME TO MY HOLY WORDS, MY CHILDREN, FOR THEY ARE YOUR PILLOW OF COMFORT AND HOPE.

COME TO MY HOLY WORDS, DEAR CHILDREN, FOR THEY REVEAL EVERYTHING ABOUT ME!

COME TO MY HOLY WORDS, DEAR CHILDREN, SO THAT YOU AND I MAY SOAR THROUGHOUT ETERNITY!

FOR, MY HOLY WORDS WILL CARRY YOU OVER EVERY HARDSHIP THAT ENTERS YOUR REALM OF CONTENTMENT.

I WANT THE BEST FOR ALL OF MY CHILDREN, FOR I LOVE ALL OF THEM, AND WANT THEM TO EXPERIENCE JOYOUS CELEBRATIONS DAILY.

WALK WITH ME, MY LITTLE ONES: AND EXPERIENCE THE DEPTHS OF ALL THAT I PLAN TO SHOW YOU.

DESPITE THE HARDSHIP THAT FLOWS THROUGH THE NATIONS: MY HOLY LIGHT STILL OUT SHINES SATAN'S REALM OF DARKNESS.

IN THE MIDST OF "THE FORETOLD WARS", MY LIGHT SHINES.

IN THE MIDST OF MURDERS AND ABUSE, MY LIGHT SHINES.

IN THE MIDST OF UNIMAGINABLE OCCURRENCES, MY HOLY LIGHT

SHINES.

I AM IN THE MIDST OF THE TRAGEDIES THAT HAVE ENGULFED MY CHILDREN TODAY.

FLEE TO ME, DEAR CHILDREN, FOR I AM YOUR PLACE OF REFUGE.

I WILL REVEAL TO YOU WHAT YOU MUST DO IN ORDER TO PREVENT SATAN FROM INVADING YOUR MINDS WITH HIS FILTHY IDEAS.

WHEN SATAN PLACES BAD OR NEGATIVE THOUGHTS IN YOUR MINDS, COMBAT HIM WITH PURE AND HOLY THOUGHTS AND ACTS.

FOR HOLINESS AND PURE LOVE WILL COMBAT SATAN AND HIS EVIL THOUGHTS.

SATAN PLACES THOUGHTS IN THE MINDS OF HUMAN BEINGS, WHICH CONVINCE THEM TO KILL THEMSELVES AND OTHERS.

I WILL SPEAK TO YOU PRIVATELY, SO THAT YOU WILL KNOW HOW SPECIAL YOU ARE TO YOUR HEAVENLY FATHER AND GOD.

I HAVE A PERSONAL AND SEPARATE RELATIONSHIP WITH ALL OF MY CHILDREN.

I KNOW EVERYTHING ABOUT EACH ONE OF YOU, FOR YOU ARE A SPECIAL PART OF ME.

I KNOW ALL OF YOUR CONCERNS: COME, LET US DISCUS THEM TODAY.

I WILL TELL YOU HOW TO APPROACH YOUR CONCERNS, SO THAT YOU WILL BENEFIT FROM THEM, INSTEAD OF BEING OVERWHELMED BY THEM.

I WILL WALK WITH YOU THROUGH EVERY EXPERIENCE THAT YOU ENCOUNTER, SO THAT YOU WILL NOT FEEL THE PRESENCE OF LONELINESS.

FOR, I AM THE LORD, YOUR ETERNAL GOD.

I AM HE THAT WATCHES OVER YOU THROUGHOUT THE DAY.

I AM HE THAT CARES FOR YOUR NEEDS.

I AM HE THAT WATCHES OVER YOUR CHILDREN WHEN YOU ARE NOT AROUND.

I AM HE THAT CONSTANTLY FIGHTS THE DEVIL AND HIS EVIL SERVANTS AS THEY HARM YOUR CHILDREN AND LOVED ONES.

I AM HE WHO WILL NEVER ABANDON YOU.

I AM HE WHO RECEIVES YOU AGAIN, WHEN YOU ABANDON ME:

FOR, I AM A FORGIVING GOD AND FATHER.

I HAVE FULFILLED MY HOLY PROMISES TO THOSE WHO HAVE TRUSTED ME OVER THE YEARS.

FOR I AM NOT A LIAR! WHAT I ORDAIN; COMES TO PASS AT "MY APPOINTED TIME", NOT MANKIND'S TIME!

"MY HOLY WORD IS MY FULFILLED PROMISE".

I AM DIVINE ORDER!

EVERYTHING COMES INTO EXISTENCE BY MY APPROVAL AND COMMAND.

THE EVILS THAT ENTER THE REALM OF EARTH'S INHABITANTS ARE WORKS OF SATAN, OUR ENEMY.

I DO NOT AGREE WITH THE EVILS THAT HE UNLEASHES DAILY, IN THE MIDST OF MY VULNERABLE CHILDREN.

HIS DAY OF DESTRUCTION IS COMING TO A LONG WAITED FOR END,

FOR MY RETURN DRAWS NEAR!

MY PROMISE TO REMOVE HIM FROM THE FACE OF EARTH WILL BE FULFILLED.

HOLD ON TO ME, MY CHILDREN, FOR OUR DAY OF CELEBRATION IS STANDING NEAR!

WE WILL WALK THE STREETS WITHOUT FEAR OR HARM.

WE WILL TRUST STRANGERS AGAIN!

WE WILL BE ABLE TO SEND OUR CHILDREN TO PLACES WHERE POTENTIAL HARM EXISTS.

WE WILL BE ABLE TO LOOK FORWARD TO ANOTHER YEAR WITHOUT DOUBT OR FEAR.

FOR MY HOLY PROMISE WILL COME TO PASS: THERE WILL BE PEACE IN MY VALLEY OF LOVE, AGAIN.

WE WILL WALK IN THE MIDST OF MY PARADISE ON EARTH, AGAIN.

I REMEMBER MY CHILDREN; ADAM AND EVE, BEFORE THEY FELL FROM MY GRACE.

I REMEMBER THE LOVE THAT FLOWED THROUGH OUR PEACEFUL GARDEN.

I REMEMBER WHEN THEY TRUSTED ME. I REMEMBER WHEN THEY OBEYED MY COMMANDS.

BUT, THAT IS THE PAST: I HAVE RESTORED THINGS THROUGH BELOVED AND ONLY BEGOTTEN SON (THE LORD JESUS).

I HAVE MADE ALL THINGS NEW THROUGH "HIS SACRIFICIAL ACT" (THE CRUCIFIXION).

I HAVE PARDONED MY DISOBEDIENT CHILDREN THROUGH "HIS GENEROUS ACT OF LOVE" (THE CRUCIFIXION).

I HAVE PARDONED THE SIN OF ADAM AND EVE.

BUT I WILL NEVER PARDON SATAN, THE DEVIL!

FOR HE HAS USED HIS LIMITED INFLUENCE OVER MY WEAK CHILDREN (ADAM AND EVE): HE TRIED TO TURN THEM AGAINST ME.

HE IS THE FATHER AND SOURCE OF DISOBEDIENCE. HE IS DOOMED.

I AM LOOKING FORWARD TO THE GOOD TIMES AGAIN, WHEN DIVINE PURE LOVE RULED THE HEAVENS AND THE EARTH.

I AM LOOKING FORWARD TO SPENDING ETERNITY WITH ADAM AND EVE AND MY OTHER REPENTANT CHILDREN.

I AM LOOKING FORWARD TO REJOICING WITH YOU, AGAIN!

ALLELUIA!!!

EPILOGUE

MY WORD: MY MESSAGE: MY PROMISE: ME!!!

BOOK FIVE

THE VICTORY IS "OURS", SAY'S THE LORD
(THE SEQUEL)

BY:

BARBARA ANN MARY MACK

COMPOSED MAY 23, 2011 AT 5:23 P.M.

DEDICATION

TO ALMIGHTY GOD, "THE VISIBLE ONE"

ACKNOWLEDGMENT

"GREATNESS (ALMIGHTY GOD) HAS EMITTED HIS HOLY PRESENCE AGAIN", THROUGH THE WRITINGS WITHIN BOOK **"ONE HUNDRED AND NINETY-ONE".**

I WILL BOW CONTINUOUSLY IN THE PRESENCE OF "GREATNESS" (ALMIGHTY GOD)

BARBARA ANN MARY MACK

PROLOGUE

"VICTORY" (THE LORD JESUS) ENTERS THE GATES OF COMPLETION AS HE UNITES WITH HIS WARRIORS (THE BELIEVERS; THE FAITHFUL ONES, THE OBEDIENT ONES) IN THE PRESENCE OF GOD, THE FATHER.

"VICTORY" (THE LORD JESUS) SALUTES "HIS GREAT FATHER AND GOD", AS HE PRESENTS THE SOULS OF THE CHOSEN FEW.

"VICTORY" (THE LORD JESUS) BOWS IN "THE PRESENCE OF HIS LOVING AND FAITHFUL FATHER", AS HE REVEAL THE SOULS OF THEIR INVITED GUESTS.

REJOICE, O HEAVENLY KING (THE LORD JESUS), FOR "YOUR FAITHFUL FLOCK" WILL LIVE AND REIGN WITH YOU, IN THE PRESENCE OF GOD, OUR FATHER, THROUGHOUT ETERNITY!

FOR YOU HAVE FOUGHT "THE BATTLE OF A TRIUMPHANT KING", THROUGHOUT OUR LIFE TIMES.

YOU, O "FAITHFUL LORD AND GOD" (JESUS), DESERVE CONTINUOUS HONOR AND GLORY, BECAUSE YOU HAVE EXPRESSED "HOLY LOYALTY TO YOUR FATHER AND GOD", IN THE PRESENCE OF THE WORLD AND SATAN.

WITNESS THE VICTORY

ALMIGHTY GOD SPEAKING

1. WITNESS "THE VICTORY" THAT SURROUNDS THOSE WHOM I HAVE CALLED TO REPRESENT ME TODAY. WITNESS THE VICTORY THAT FLOWS IN THE MIDST OF HARMS WAY.

2. WITNESS "THE VICTORY" THAT SURROUNDS MY BIRTH: AS I ENLIGHTEN MY CHILDREN WITH THE PRESENCE OF MY LOVE ON EARTH.

3. I AM WITH YOU, DEAR CHILDREN, AS YOU KNEEL AND PRAY: I AM SURROUNDING MY BLESSED ONES THROUGHOUT THE DAY.

4. "VICTORY" IS THE SONG THAT ALL NATIONS WILL SING, AS THEY GATHER AROUND "THE THRONE OF THEIR HEAVENLY KING" (ALMIGHTY GOD).

BARBARA SPEAKING

5. SING, LORD JESUS, SING, FOR THE VICTORY IS YOURS! SING, O PRECIOUS SON OF GOD, AS YOUR WALK THROUGH OUR DOORS.

6. I WILL FIGHT WITH YOU, LORD JESUS, AS WE BATTLE FOR THE SOULS OF YOUR LOVED ONES: WE WILL DEFEAT THE EVIL SPIRITS, SO THAT THEY WILL NOT HARM YOUR DAUGHTERS AND SONS.

7. "THE VICTORY IS OURS TODAY. O SOVEREIGN AND HOLY KING":

8. WE WILL DANCE IN THE STREETS OF VICTORY, AS WE SHOUT AND SING.

9. WE WILL SING SONGS OF PRAISE THAT REACH THE MOUNTAINS TOP: WE WILL EXPRESS "THE TUNES OF TRIUMPH", AS WE WITNESS THE DEFEAT OF SATAN'S EVIL STOCK!

10. HIS (SATAN) STOCK IS PLENTY; CAUSING DAMAGE TO EVERY NATION: BEWARE OF HIS SERVANTS, WHO DESIRE TO STEAL MY GREAT CREATION.

ALMIGHTY GOD SPEAKING

11. RUN TO ME, DEAR CHILDREN, SO THAT SATAN WILL NOT STEAL YOUR ETERNAL SOULS, MY LOVE: RUN, INTO "THE ARMS OF YOUR SAVING GOD".

12. INTO "MY HEAVENLY KINGDOM" WE WILL DINE: AROUND "MY TABLE OF PLENTY", THROUGHOUT THE REALM OF TIME.

13. DANCE IN "THE PRESENCE OF THE VICTORIOUS ONE" (ALMIGHTY GOD), WITH YOUR ARMS OPEN WIDE: DANCE IN "THE PRESENCE OF THE HOLY TRINITY UNTIL THE END OF TIME".

14. EVERY NATION WILL ENJOY "MY BREAD OF LIFE", AS THEY EAT "MY WORDS OF LOVE", THAT ARE DELIVERED BY "MY SPIRITUAL WIFE" (BARBARA).

15. EAT FROM MY TABLE OF PLENTY IN THE PRESENCE OF GOD, OUR FATHER, AND LORD": ENJOY "THE GOODNESS OF THE HOLY ONE", AS WE SING ON ONE ACCORD.

16. "THE SONGS OF VICTORY WILL FLOW THROUGH MY REALM OF LOVE": AS YOU REJOICE IN "THE PRESENCE OF GOD'S HOLY DOVE" (SPIRIT).

BARBARA SPEAKING

17. "THE SOUNDS OF TRIUMPH HAVE DESCENDED FROM ABOVE"; MIXED WITH "THE GOODNESS OF GOD'S SACRED LOVE".

18. I CAN HEAR "THE WORDS THAT FLOW FROM THE MOUTH OF OUR HEAVENLY FATHER AND KING": I CAN HEAR "THE SONGS OF PRAISE THAT HIS HEAVENLY CHOIR SINGS".

19. WE WILL JOIN "YOUR CHOIR OF LOVE, O GREAT AND SOVEREIGN ONE" (GOD, THE FATHER): AS YOU REJOICE WITH US, AND YOUR ONLY BEGOTTEN SON (THE LORD JESUS).

20. "VICTORY" (THE LORD JESUS) WILL TAKE HIS PLACE AT "YOUR TABLE OF LOVE": AS HE DINES IN "THE PRESENCE OF THE HOLY DOVE".

21. LIFT US UP, LORD JESUS, IN "THE PRESENCE OF HOLY VICTORY AND FAME": SO THAT WE MAY PROCLAIM "THE GOODNESS OF YOUR HOLY NAME".

22. "VICTORY WILL UNITE WITH SWEET PEACE, AS WE BOW IN YOUR HOLY PRESENCE", SO THAT WE THAT WE MAY BECOME ENGULFED BY "YOUR SPIRITUAL GREATNESS".

23. I WILL SHARE "THE GOODNESS OF MY LOVING KING OF PEACE", AS I ENJOY "THE BOUNTIFUL BLESSINGS THAT HE CONSTANTLY RELEASE".

24. INTO "THE HANDS OF ALMIGHTY GOD" I WILL REST, AS I STRIVE TO PAST "HIS PAST HIS VICTORIOUS TEST".

25. A TEST THE REVEAL MY LOVE AND FAITH; FOR ALL OF GOD'S CHILDREN WHO LONG TO SEE HIS GLORIOUS FACE.

26. I WILL EXPRESS MY FAITH IN THE LORD EVERY DAY AND NIGHT; AS I REACH FOR THE STRENGTH THAT FLOWS FROM "HIS HOLY LIGHT".

27. MY LOVE FOR GOD'S CHILDREN FLOWS FROM HIS INDWELLING SPIRIT. I WILL SING OF THE OF OUR ETERNAL GOD, SO THAT ALL OF CREATION MAY HEAR IT.

BOOK SIX

I HAVE SHARED YOUR HOLY CROSS, MY LORD

BY:

BARBARA ANN MARY MACK

COMPOSED MAY 23, 2011

DEDICATION

I DEDICATE THIS BOOK OF LOVE TO "MY SOVEREIGN SPOUSE AND GOD" (THE LORD, JESUS).

ACKNOWLEDGMENT

MY LORD: I PRAISE YOU FOR ALLOWING "YOUR HUMBLE SERVANT", BARBARA ANN MARY MACK, THE PRIVILEGE AND HONOR TO COMPOSE BOOK "**ONE HUNDRED AND NINETY-TWO**, IN THE PRESENCE AND COMPANY OF YOUR CHOSEN FLOCK OF LOVE TODAY.

PROLOGUE

THE HOLY SPIRIT SPEAKS OF THE LORD'S BRIDE (BARBARA)

THE SPIRIT OF THE BRIDE (BARBARA) OF THE GREAT LORD JESUS, CRIES OUT, AS SHE SHARES "HIS CROSS OF LOVE" WITH HIM.

THE SPIRIT OF THE LAMB'S BRIDE (BARBARA) CRIES OUT, AS SHE CLINGS TO "THE BEING OF HER HOLY SPOUSE AND GOD" (THE LORD JESUS).

THE SPIRIT OF THE BRIDE (BARBARA) SHARES THE PAIN THAT COMES WITH A "DIVINE SACRIFICIAL ACT OF LOVE" (SERVITUDE UNTO ALMIGHTY GOD AND HIS CHILDREN).

THE SPIRIT OF THE BRIDE OF THE HOLY AND GREAT TRINITY, REACHES OUT TO GOD'S CHOSEN FLOCK, AS SHE CLINGS TO "THE BEING OF THE CRUCIFIED KING" (THE LORD JESUS).

THE SPIRIT OF THE HOLY ONE'S (ALMIGHTY GOD) BRIDE (BARBARA), TRUSTS IN "THE GOODNESS OF GOD, THE FATHER AND HIS ONLY BEGOTTEN SON" (THE LORD, JESUS).

THE SPIRIT OF THE BRIDE (BARBARA) CALLS OUT TO THE WANDERING SHEEP OF "THE CRUCIFIED LORD, JESUS".

THE SPIRIT OF THE BRIDE (BARBARA) OF CHRIST JESUS, FULFILLS HER DIVINE TASK WITH THE GUIDANCE AND STRENGTH OF "THE HOLY SPIRIT" (ALMIGHTY GOD).

THE SPIRIT OF THE LORD'S BRIDE (BARBARA) REJOICES, AS SHE COMPLETES HER "DIVINE SACRIFICIAL ACT OF LOVE" IN THE

PRESENCE OF THE WORLD.

THE SPIRIT OF THE LORD'S BRIDE (BARBARA) REJOICES THROUGHOUT ETERNITY, IN THE PRESENCE OF "THE HOLY ONE" (ALMIGHTY GOD) AND "HIS GREAT CREATION OF LOVE" (HUMAN BEINGS).

ALLELUIA! O "VICTORIOUS ONES" (THE LORD JESUS AND BARBARA); ALLELUIA!!!

CHAPTER ONE

ENTER, MY DAUGHTER: MY CONDUIT

THE HOLY SPIRIT SPEAKING

BEHOLD: SOMETHING VERY "UNIQUE" AND "PROFOUND" HAS ENTERED THIS WORLD, AGAIN.

BEHOLD: "THE BRIDE (BARBARA) OF THE CRUCIFIED LORD JESUS", HAS ENTERED THIS WORLD OF CONFUSION AND DESPAIR, AT "HIS HOLY COMMAND AND LOVE FOR HIS LOST AND WANDERING FLOCK.

BEHOLD: "THE PROPHECY HAS ENTERED THIS REALM OF APPOINTED TIME IN HISTORY".

BEHOLD: "THE DIVINE ACT OF LOVE CONTINUES THROUGH HIS CHOSEN AND SACRIFICIAL BRIDE" (BARBARA ANN MARY MACK).

BEHOLD: "THE GIFT (BARBARA) FROM THE LORD JESUS CHRIST".

BARBARA SPEAKING TO THE LORD

MY LORD: "THE LOVE OF YOUR HOLY CROSS"-HAS CARRIED ME OVER "THE RIVERS OF PHYSICAL AND SPIRITUAL PAIN".

CHOSEN AND FORM BY YOU, AND THROUGH YOU; I AM GIVEN "THE GRACE AND STAMINA OF ONE WHO POSSESSES A FRAGMENT OF YOUR HOLY AND ETERNAL ESSENCE OF LOVE".

THE BRIDE (BARBARA) SPEAKS

BARBARA SPEAKING TO THE LORD, JESUS

SWEET RAIN DROPS FROM HEAVEN ACCOMPANY "THE WORDS OF OUR PERFECT SAVIOR AND GOD, THE LORD JESUS", DAILY, AS I WATCH THROUGH "MY WINDOWS OF LOVE".

THE SWEET MELODIES THE EMIT "SANCTIFIED LOVE" EMERGE FROM THE BEING OF MY PERFECT SAVIOR AND GOD (THE LORD JESUS).

THE BLOSSOMED FLOWERS EMIT THE RADIANCE OF THEIR CREATOR AND GOD (THE LORD JESUS).

THE SWEET FRAGRANCE THAT FLOWS FROM THE LILLIES OF THE FIELDS, REJOICES IN THE PRESENCE OF ITS CREATOR AND GOD (THE LORD JESUS).

THE HOLINESS THAT SURROUNDS THE BIRTH OF YOUR SACRED CROSS, IS ENVELOPED IN THE SWEETNESS OF THE HEAVENLY TUNES, O SACRIFICIAL LAMB OF ALMIGHTY GOD, OUR FATHER.

BARBARA SPEAKS TO THE SWEET TUNES FROM HEAVEN

REJOICE! O SWEET TUNES, AS YOU EMBRACE "THE SAVIOR (THE LORD JESUS) OF THE WORLD, AS I SHARE HIS HOLY CROSS OF LOVE".

REJOICE! O SWEET MELODIES FROM HEAVEN, AS I DANCE WITH "MY LORD'S SANCTIFIED CROSS OF LOVE"!

BOW IN "THE PRESENCE OF GREATNESS" (THE LORD JESUS) AS HE ENTERS "THE HOLY DANCE FLOOR WITH HIS INVITED GUESTS".

BARBARA SPEAKING TO THE LORD JESUS

DANCE! LORD JESUS, DANCE!

DANCE IN THE COMPANY OF "YOUR REJOICING FLOCK", FOR THEY ACKNOWLEDGE "YOUR HOLY ETERNAL PRESENCE" TODAY!

WE WILL SHARE YOUR CROSS-OF LOVE AS WE PROCLAIM "THE GOOD NEWS OF YOUR HOLY GOSPEL, LORD JESUS".

BARBARA SPEAKING TO GOD'S CREATION

LIFT UP YOUR VOICES IN PRAISE, ALL YE LANDS OF PLENTY! FOR "ALMIGHTY GOD, THE FATHER, HAS SENT HIS HOLY ESSENCE (THE LORD JESUS) TO DWELL IN YOUR MIDST, THROUGH HIS CHOSEN BRIDE (BARBARA) AND SERVANT OF LOVE".

LIFT UP YOUR VOICES IN PRAISE, O GREAT MOUNTAINS THAT COVER THE EARTH! FOR "THE LORD JESUS HAS DESCENDED IN YOUR MIDST TODAY".

GIVE HIM "CONTINUOUS PRAISE", O SWEET HILLS THAT BOW IN CHRIST'S HOLY PRESENCE DAILY: FOR HE IS "KING OF KINGS, AND LORD OF LORD!

GIVE HIM PRAISE AND ACKNOWLEDGMENT, O RUSHING WATERS THAT COVER THE EARTH!

GIVE HIM PRAISE! O VALLEYS THAT REVEAL APPRECIATION AND ALLEGIANCE, FOR "HE REIGNS IN OUR MIDST TODAY"!!!

ROLL OUT THE FINEST CARPET, AND SALUTE OUR GREAT KING, FOR HE HAS COMPLETED "HIS SACRED ACT OF LOVE" (THE CRUCIFIXION).

ROLL OUT THE CARPET OF LOVE, FOR ALMIGHTY GOD (THE LORD JESUS) HAS DEFEATED THE REALM (SATAN) THAT PRODUCES FEAR AND BETRAYAL.

BOOK SEVEN

VARIOUS POEMS AND SAYINGS

BY:

BARBARA ANN MARY MACK

TO KEN, FROM HIS EXTENDED FAMILY

TO OUR BELOVED GOOD SHEPHERD AND FRIEND (FATHER KENNETH CHARLES BRABAZON, JR.):

YOU WILL REMAIN IN OUR BASKET OF CONTINUOUS PRAYERS, BECAUSE YOU REPRESENT JESUS, OUR GOOD AND FIRST SHEPHERD.

YOU HAVE FOLLOWED "THE FOOTSTEPS OF ALFA AND OMEGA" (OUR GOOD SHEPHERD, THE LORD JESUS) SINCE YOUR YOUTH.

THE GATES OF HEAVEN HAVE OPENED AND EMBRACED YOUR MINISTRY. GO FORTH, MY SPIRITUAL SON, AND PROCLAIM THE GOOD NEWS OF OUR GREAT AND HOLY GOD.

WITH GOD'S ETERNAL BLESSINGS AND CARE,

YOUR SPIRITUAL MOTHER AND PRAYER WARRIOR, BARBARA ANN MARY MACK

WE ARE SO PROUD OF YOU FOR FOLLOWING THE PATH THAT THE LORD CHOSE YOU TO TAKE. WE KNOW THAT YOU WILL CONTINUE TO MAKE THE LORD PROUD FIRST AND US AS WELL. MAY YOU CONTINUE TO GROW IN YOUR LOVE OF THE LORD AND YOUR NEW PRIESTLY DUTIES.

WITH GOD'S ETERNAL LOVE,

LATOYA ROBINSON (BARBARA'S DAUGHTER)

I'LL KEEP YOU IN MY PRAYERS.

AMYA TURPIN (LA TOYA'S DAUGHTER)

TO FR. CRAIG, MY SON: MY BELOVED ONE, SAYS THE LORD JESUS

TO BLESSED AND HOLY CRAIG:

I HAVE WASHED YOUR FEET

I HAVE WASHED YOUR HOLY FEET TODAY, FOR THEY REPRESENT MINE.

I HAVE CAREFULLY GUIDED YOUR CHOSEN FEET, SO THAT THEY WOULD LEAD OTHERS TO ME.

I HAVE BATHED YOUR FEET IN "THE SPIRIT OF THE HOLY TRINITY", FOR YOU REPRESENT ME.

I HAVE BATHED YOUR FEET IN "THE WATERS THAT FLOW FROM MY WELL OF LOVE", SO THAT THEY WILL WALK IN THE DIRECTION OF DIVINE LOVE.

I HAVE BATHED YOUR FEET, O CHOSEN SON, RISE AND EXHIBIT ME!

I WILL LEAD YOU IN THE DIRECTION OF "DIVINE TRUTH", SO THAT "MY WORDS AND ESSENCE" WILL PERMEATE YOUR SOUL DAILY.

WALK WITH ME, O CHOSEN SON, SO THAT "MY ESSENCE" MAY IGNITE THOSE WHOM YOU MEET.

WALK WITH ME, O CHOSEN AND BLESSED SON, THROUGHOUT ETERNITY.

FOR, YOUR HOLY FEET REPRESENT YOUR RISEN LORD: YOUR VICTORIOUS KING: YOUR OBEDIENT BROTHER (THE LORD JESUS): AND YOUR OMNIPOTENT GOD.

WALK WITH ME, O CHOSEN SON; IN THE PRESENCE OF THE WORLD!

FOR, I HAVE RISEN WITHIN YOU TODAY!!! ALLELUIA!

THUS SAYS, THE LORD

HAPPY RESURRECTION DAY!!!

LET THE CELEBRATION BEGIN, CRAIG

ROLL OUT THE CARPET!

ENTER THE DANCE!

GRAB YOUR NEIGHBOR, AND CELEBRATE TODAY:

FOR CHRIST JESUS HAS TAKEN THE STAND IN THE PRESENCE

OF THE WORLD AGAIN!

WITNESS "HIS HOLY PRESENCE" IN YOUR MIDST, AS YOU RISE WITH

"THE VICTORIOUS ONE" (THE LORD JESUS).

WITNESS "HIS HOLY PRESENCE", AS HE PROCLAIMS "VICTORY OF THE REALM OF DECEIT AND DESTRUCTION" AGAIN.

WITNESS "THE PRESENCE OF THE RESURRECTED ONE" (THE LORD JESUS), AS HE APPROACHES YOUR CHOSEN BEING.

RISE WITH "THE VICTORIOUS KING", AS HE WALTZES IN THE PRESENCE OF GOD, OUR FATHER.

DANCE! LORD JESUS, DANCE!

EXHIBIT "THE PRESENCE OF THE TRIUMPHANT KING":

FOR OUR HEAVENLY FATHER IS WELL-PLEASED AGAIN!

DANCE! LORD JESUS, DANCE!

DANCE WITH "YOUR VICTORIOUS BRIDE" (BARBARA):

FOR YOU HAVE RISEN AGAIN, THROUGH HER OBEDIENT PRESENCE!

THUS SAYS, BARBARA ANN MARY MACK

JOIN OUR CELEBRATION TODAY, FOR I HAVE COME BACK TO CELEBRATE WITH YOU!!!

I WILL DANCE IN THE PRESENCE OF THE WORLD TODAY, FOR I HAVE RISEN AGAIN!!! ALLELUIA!!!

THUS SAYS, THE LORD!

BEHOLD! "I MAKE ALL THINGS NEW, SAYS THE LORD!"

WHERE IS THE REVERENCE THAT ONCE EXISTED IN MY CHURCHES?

TODAY, I HWVE SEARCHED AND SEARCHED, BUT, I COULD NOT FIND A CHURCH THAT REVERED ME. I WAS PRESENT: I WAS WITHIN THEIR SIGHT: THEY COULD TOUCH ME: SOME OF THEM DID TOUCH ME; BUT THEY KNEW ME NOT.

I SAT IN THEIR PEWS FOR YEARS, BUT THEY DID NOT RECOGNIZE ME. I SPOKE THE WORDS THAT ONLY I COULD SPEAK: BUT, THEY FAILED TO ACKNOWLEDGE ME.

I HAVE WEPT IN THEIR PRESENCE, BECAUSE THEY EXHIBITED IRREVERENCE TOWARD THE HOLY ONE (ALMIGHTY GOD); THEIR CREATOR.

I WILL RETURN TO MY HOME, WHERE REVERENCE ENCOMPASSES MY ESSENCE.

WHERE? OH WHERE ARE YOU, SWEET REVERENCE? WHERE DO YOU HIDE TODAY?

FOR, I SEEK YOU, DEAR REVERENCE: I SEEK YOU IN VAIN!

THUS SAYS, THE LORD

"BEHOLD! I HAVE RETURNED TO REVIVE REVERENCE FOR ALMIGHTY GOD IN THE CHURCHES!"

THUS SAYS, THE LORD ALMIGHTY!!!

O WHAT A DAY OF CELEBRATION

FOR IT WAS NOT SO LONG AGO, THAT "THE MASTER (THE LORD JESUS) ENTERED OUR TANGIBLE REALM AGAIN".

LET US LIFT UP OUR VOICES IN "CONTINUOUS PRAISE", AS WE GREET "THE ALLELUIAS THAT SURROUND HIS HOLY ESSENCE ON EARTH TODAY"!!!

REJOICE, O HEAVEN SENT ONE (THE LORD JESUS), FOR "YOUR HOLY PRESENCE" IS WELCOMED IN OUR MIDST TODAY!!!

LET THE "ALLELUIAS DANCE IN THE PRESENCE OF GOD, OUR FATHER, AS WE BOW WITH GRATITUDE AND LOVE"!

WALK WITH US, O WELCOMED ALLELUIAS, AS WE GREET OUR VICTORIOUS KING (THE LORD JESUS) TODAY!

FOR HE EXHIBITS "DIVINE LOVE", "TRIUMPH", "VICTORY", "GLORY", "SOVEREIGNTY", "LORDSHIP", "TRANQUILITY", "REFUGE" AND "CONTINUOUS HOPE"!

REJOICE WITH GLADNESS IN YOUR HEART, O BELOVED ONE, FOR HE HAS ENTERED!!! ALLELUIA!!!

SHELTER ME FROM THE WORLD AND ITS CRUELTY

MY ESSENCE WEEPS OVER THE KNOWLEDGE OF PAIN AND CRUELTY THAT ENCOMPASS MY EARTHLY BROTHERS AND SISTERS.

HELP THEM! DEAR LORD. RELEAVE ME FROM THE AGONY THAT ENCOMPASSES MY EMPATHETIC SOUL: FOR THE KNOWLEDGE OF THE SUFFERING THAT YOUR CHILDREN ARE SUBJECTED TO IS HEAVY ON MY HEART.

RELIEVE ME, DEAR LORD, FROM THE PAIN THAT IS INFLICTED ON US

(BARBARA AND GOD'S CHILDREN): FOR YOU HAVE REVEAL TO ME THE HARDSHIP AND CRUELTY THAT SURROUND YOUR VULNERABLE CHILDREN TODAY.

HELP US, DEAR LORD, FOR THE PAIN IS WEIGHING ME DOWN.

EMPATHY HAS NO COMPARISON, TO ACTUALLY

WITNESSING CRUELTY.

HELP US, DEAR LORD, FOR YOUR CHILDREN ARE WORTH IT!

THE WEIGHT OF THE SUFFERING ONES IS VERY HEAVY ON MY HEART

WILL YOU CARRY ME? FOR I HAVE BECOME VERY WEAK WITH SORROW.

THE KNOWLEDGE OF PAIN THAT OVERPOWERS THE CAPTURED ONES HAS WEAKENED MY ENTIRE ESSENCE.

WILL YOU CARRY ME, SO THAT I MAY MAINTAIN MY STANCE IN THE BATTLE AND VIGIL AGAINST THE REALM (SATAN) THAT CAUSES GREAT SUFFERING TO GOD'S VULNERABLE ONES?

WILL YOU CARRY ME? O BELOVED ONE, FOR THE STRAIN OF THE SUFFERING AND ABUSED ONES IS VERY HEAVY TODAY!

SOME PEOPLE BELIEVE THAT ALMIGHTY GOD SITS IDLE; AND WITHOUT CARE AS HIS LITTLE CHILDREN ARE BEING ABUSED AND/OR MURDERED.

BUT, I CAN ATTEST TO THE GREAT SUFFERING THAT BEARS DOWN ON THE CREATOR AND GOD OF HUMAN LIFE. THE LORD WEEPS AT THE SIGHT OF INFLICTION THAT OVERPOWERS THE ABUSED ONES.

WILL YOU CARRY US (THE LORD AND BARBARA) TODAY? O BELOVED ONE, FOR THE WEIGHT OF THE SUFFERING ONES IS VERY HEAVY ON OUR (THE LORD AND BARBARA) HEART.

CARRY US, O BELOVED ONE (CRAIG, GOD'S CHOSEN SON), FOR WE (THE LORD AND BARBARA) NEED YOU TODAY.

BARBARA ANN MARY MACK (THE SORROWFUL ONE)

THE [FENCE] THAT SURROUNDS YOU DAILY

LIKE THE HARSH WINDS AND RAIN THAT BEAT AGAINST THE WEAK WINDOWS, SATAN ATTEMPTS TO REACH YOU:

BUT WE (THE LORD AND ME) ARE THE WINDOW THAT PROTECTS YOU FROM THE HARSH DARTS THAT SATAN INTENDS FOR YOU. WE (THE LORD AND ME) ARE THE [FENCE] THAT SURROUNDS YOU DAILY:

MAINTAIN YOUR COMPOSURE, FOR I (THE LORD AND ME) WILL CONQUER SATAN'S DARTS.

WE (THE LORD AND ME) ARE ONE.

AS WE SHARE THE TOMB WITH CHRIST JESUS

AS WE (CRAIG AND BARBARA) ENTER "THE PROMISED TOMB" WITH OUR OBEDIENT SAVIOR AND GOD (THE LORD JESUS), WE WILL BOW IN THE PRESENCE OF GOD, OUR (THE LORD JESUS, CRAIG AND BARBARA) FATHER.

AS WE ENTER THE TOMB WITH CHRIST JESUS, WE WILL ENCOMPASS HIS BRUISED AND LIFELESS BODY WITH OUR LOVE.

AS WE ENTER THE TOMB WITH CHRIST JESUS, OUR HYMNS OF PRAISE SERVE AS A PILLOW FOR HIS BRUISED AND LIFELESS HEAD.

AS WE ENTER THE TOMB WITH CHRIST JESUS, WE WILL CARRY HIS BELOVED BODY TO ITS RESTING PLACE.

AS WE ENTER THE TOMB WITH CHRIST JESUS, OUR MELODIOUS SONGS UPLIFT HIS ETERNAL SPIRIT.

AS WE ENTER THE TOMB WITH CHRIST JESUS, WE WILL OFFER OUR PRESENCE, AS A SHIELD AGAINST THE EVIL SPIRITS THAT ARE ANGRY OVER "HIS TRIUMPHANT ACT OF LOVE" (THE CRUCIFIXION).

SING "YOUR SONG OF VICTORY", O CRUCIFIED ONE (THE LORD JESUS), AS WE (CRAIG AND BARBARA) BOW IN "YOUR ROYAL AND HOLY PRESENCE"!

"VICTORY AND FAME" ENTER THE TOMB OF CHRIST JESUS, AS A SIGN OF "HIS ACT OF OBEDIENCE UNTO GOD, OUR FATHER".

"VICTORY AND FAME" ENTER THE TOMB OF CHRIST JESUS, AS HE LAY ON THE CARVED STONE.

"VICTORY AND FAME" SURROUND THE BODY OF "THE CRUCIFIED KING (THE LORD JESUS) OF KINGS".

"PEACE AND TRANQUILITY" ENCOMPASS THE ESSENCE OF "THE PRINCE (THE LORD JESUS) OF SACRED PEACE".

"ALLEGIANCE AND DEVOTION" DANCE IN THE PRESENCE OF "THE SOVEREIGN ONE" (THE LORD JESUS).

CRAIG AND BARBARA DANCE TO THE BEAT OF "VICTORY", IN THE TOMB OF OUR CRUCIFIED LORD.

REJOICE WITH US (CRAIG AND BARBARA), O "VICTORIOUS KING" (THE LORD JESUS), FOR WE (THE LORD JESUS, CRAIG AND BARBARA) HAVE "COMPLETED THE WILL OF GOD,

OUR FATHER, AGAIN"!

REJOICE WITH US (CRAIG AND BARBARA), O HEAVEN SENT ONE (THE CRUCIFIED LORD JESUS), FOR WE (THE LORD JESUS, CRAIG AND BARBARA) ARE "THE SURVIVORS"!

"THE ALLELUIAS SURROUND US" (THE LORD JESUS, CRAIG AND BARBARA), AS WE REST IN "THE SACRED TOMB OF CHRIST JESUS".

AMEN!!!

MY HEART WEEPS WITH YOURS

CRADLED WITHIN YOUR HEART BEFORE THE REALM OF TIME: LIES
THE HEART THAT WEEPS WITH YOURS.

WITHIN THE DEPTH OF YOUR RESTLESS SOUL: LIES
THE HEART THAT WEEPS WITH YOURS.

IN THE CENTER OF YOUR WELL OF LOVE: LIES
THE HEART THAT WEEPS WITH YOURS.

SNUGGLED WITHIN THE GATES OF PARADISE: LIES
THE HEART THAT WEEPS WITH YOURS.

BELOW THE HEAVENS THAT WERE FORMED BY LOVE (ALMIGHTY GOD) LIES THE
HEART THAT WEEPS WITH YOURS.

I SEARCH DAILY WITHIN THE REALM THAT HIDES, THE HEART THAT WEEPS WITH
MINE.

WE WILL WEEP NO MORE, O BELOVED HEART, BECAUSE THE SUN HAS RELEASED
ITS RADIANCE, BY THE POWER OF OUR CREATOR AND GOD.

WE WILL WEEP NO MORE, O BELOVED OF MINE, FOR OUR HAPPINESS HAS BEEN
RELEASED BY THE ORIGIN (ALMIGHTY GOD) OF "THE APPOINTED TIME"!

COMPOSED APRIL 13, 2011 AROUND 11:20 P.M.-11:40 P.M

BARBARA ANN MARY MACK

CARRY ME HOME

THERE'S A PLACE:
MY REFUGE: MY DESTINATION!

IS IT NEAR?
IS IT WITHIN MY REALM OF TOUCH?

I AM SO TIRED! I AM SPIRITUALLY AND PHYSICALLY EXHAUSTED!

REST! SWEET, SWEET, REST!

DOES IT EXIST FOR ME?
DOES IT EXIST FOR YOU?
DOES IT EXIST FOR OUR CREATOR AND GOD?

IS IT NEAR? IS IT WITHIN MY REALM OF TOUCH?
IS IT WITH YOU?

CARRY ME HOME, O SWEET REALM THAT MY WEARY BEING SEARCHES FOR DAILY!

CARRY ME TO MY PLACE OF REFUGE!

IS IT NEAR?
IS IT WITH YOU?

CARRY ME HOME, O SWEET GATES THAT I LONG TO ENTER!
CARRY ME TO MY PLACE OF CONTINUOUS TRANQUILITY!

IS IT NEAR?
IS IT WITHIN MY REALM OF TOUCH?
IS IT WITHIN MY REALM OF HOPE?

MORE THAN A WOMAN

MANY PEOPLE KNOW OF, AND BELIEVE IN MY POSITION, **"MORE THAN A WOMAN"**!

MANY, WHOM I HAVE SPOKEN WITH, AND HAVE SHARED MY GOD REVEALED MESSAGES TO,

HAVE GRASPED THE SEVERITY AND UNDERSTANDING OF MY POSITION AS BEING **"MORE THAN A WOMAN"**.

YESTERDAY I BEGAN WRITING BOOK #188, WHICH REVEALS MY POSITION AS BEING SOMEONE WHO IS **"MORE THAN A WOMAN"**.

O HOW MAGNIFICENT OUR GOD IS, TO HAVE REVEALED HIS HOLY PRESENCE THROUGH SOMEONE WHO IS **"MORE THAN A WOMAN"**.

SOMEONE (BARBARA, **A WOMAN**) WHO WAS SENT TO FULFILL WHAT EVE FAILED TO DO (ALLEGIANCE AND OBEDIENCE TO ALMIGHTY GOD AND ADAM, AT ALL TIMES).

ALMIGHTY GOD SENT **A WOMAN** (BARBARA ANN MARY MACK) TO PROVE TO SATAN THAT GOD'S GIFT **(WOMAN)** TO MAN CAN BE TRUSTED AGAIN.

GOD SENT **A WOMAN** TO COMBAT AND DEFEAT SATAN AND HIS REALM OF DECEPTION AND LIMITATION.

GOD GRACES BARBARA WITH **"THE GIFT OF FORTIFICATION"** DAILY, SO THAT SATAN AND HIS REALM OF DECEPTION WILL NOT OVER POWER OR PENETRATE HER WEAKNESS.

BARBARA, GOD'S GIFT TO THE WORLD: IS **"MORE THAN A WOMAN"**!

REMEMBER ME!!!

REVERE ME!!! AND REVIVE ME!!!

"FOR, I HAVE RETURNED, TO MAKE ALL THINGS NEW, SAYS THE LORD

MY GOD: YOU ARE!

YOU ARE "GRACIOUS"!

YOU ARE "OUR PROVIDER"!

YOU ARE "OUR REFUGE"!

YOU ARE "OUR HELP IN TIMES OF NEED"!

YOU ARE "ALWAYS PRESENT", DEAR LORD!

YOU ARE "OUR ALMIGHTY GOD"!!!

YOUR "GRACE" SURROUNDS US DAILY"!

YOUR "GRACE SURROUNDS OUR BELOVED ONE (PADRE CRAIG) DAILY"!

YOUR "GRACE SUSTAINS OUR BELOVED ONE, DAILY"!

YOUR "GRACE AND STRENGTH MOVE HIM CLOSER TO ME, DAILY".

YOUR "GRACE IGNITES HIS DORMANT BEING IN THE PRESENCE OF THE WORLD".

DO NOT WEEP: FOR, I AM WITH YOU ALWAYS, SAYS BARBARA ANN MARY MACK!!!

DO NOT WEEP, O SWEET ONE WHO MELTS OUR (THE LORD AND ME) INVITING HEART!

DO NOT WEEP: FOR I AM WITH YOU TODAY!!!

TOUCH MY SPIRIT AS IT ROAMS IN YOUR WELL-LOVED MIDST.

TOUCH MY WELCOMED SPIRIT TODAY!

FOR HEAVEN (ALMIGHTY GOD) HAS OPENED HIS GATES OF LOVE AND RELEASED ME, SO THAT I MAY COMFORT YOU DAILY.

HEAVEN (ALMIGHTY GOD) HAS OPENED HIS GATES AND RELEASED HIS EXTENSION (BARBARA) OF LOVE, SO THAT I MAY CAPTURE YOUR FALLING TEARS.

DO NOT WEEP! O BELOVED ONE: FOR I AM WITH YOU ALWAYS!!!

TAKE ME AWAY

TAKE ME AWAY FROM THE CARES OF THIS WORLD:

TAKE ME AWAY FROM THE KNOWLEDGE OF INFLICTED PAIN ON MY EARTHLY CHILDREN:

TAKE ME AWAY FROM THE KNOWLEDGE OF EVIL THAT FLOWS OVER GOD'S VULNERABLE CHILDREN.

TAKE ME AWAY, O DEAR ONE, FROM THIS LIMITED BRUISED WORLD.
FOR IT EXHIBITS THE MARKS OF CRUELTY AND INFLICTED PAIN.

TAKE ME AWAY, O DEAR ONE, TO AN ISOLATED ISLAND OF BLISS.
TAKE ME AWAY, O DEAR ONE, TO THE PLACE WHERE ONLY SERENITY EXISTS.

TAKE ME AWAY, O DEAR ONE, TO YOUR SPIRITUAL SHORE:

TAKE ME AWAY, O DEAR ONE, SO THAT I WILL FEAR NO MORE!

COMPOSED APRIL 13, 2011 AT 4:55-5:00 A.M.

THE ELEGANCE OF THE WORLD

THE ELEGANCE OF THE WORLD CANNOT "TRANSCEND OR EQUATE TO THE ELEGANCE THAT EMITS FROM THE HOLY SPIRITUAL REALM", WHICH ENCOMPASSES GOD'S CHOSEN ONES (YOU AND ME).

THE ELEGANCE OF THE WORLD IS VISIBLE ONLY TO THE NAKED EYE, WHICH EMITS "LIMITATIONS AND QUESTS".

THE ELEGANCE OF THE WORLD EXHIBITS THE REALM OF SATAN'S TEMPORARY BEAUTY AND FAME.

LET US TRANSCEND THE REALM (SATAN'S WORLDLY FAME AND FORTUNE) THAT PRODUCES LIMITATIONS AND WONDERS, AS WE APPROACH "THE HOLY ONE'S (ALMIGHTY GOD) ELEGANT TERRITORY" (HEAVENLY BLISS)!

WE WILL WALK IN THE MIDST OF "SPIRITUAL ELEGANCE" ON EARTH TODAY!

WE WILL "REJOICE" IN THE ELEGANCE THAT DESCENDED FROM HEAVEN, AND CAPTURED OUR INVITING SOULS!

O SWEET SOURCE (ALMIGHTY GOD) OF SPIRITUAL ELEGANCE: PLEASE LEAD ME TO YOUR WAITING ARMS.

COMFORT ME, AS YOU COMFORT OUR BELOVED ONE (CRAIG), O SWEET ELEGANCE (ALMIGHTY GOD): AS I SOAR BENEATH YOUR HEAVENLY SKIES.

COMFORT ME, O HEAVENLY FATHER; AS MY HOLY SPIRIT "REJOICES" AS IT FLIES!

IN THE DIRECTION OF "HEAVENLY BLISS", SWEET ELEGANCE SOARS DAILY!

SURROUND ME, O SWEET ELEGANCE, AS I APPROACH "THE BLESSED TRINITY"!

COMPOSED FEBRUARY 3, 2011

WOMAN: A GIFT TO MAN

A GIFT TO MAN, SENT FROM ABOVE.

A GIFT TO MAN, THAT EXPRESSES DIVINE LOVE (ALMIGHTY GOD).

A GIFT THAT COMFORTS, SOOTHES AND HEALS:

A GIFT THAT IS SENT WITH GOD'S HOLY SEAL.

A GIFT THAT SURROUNDS HER MAN WITH CONTINUOUS PEACE:

WOMAN IS "THE GIFT THAT HEAVEN RELEASED"!

ARE YOU BLESSED WITH "THE GIFT" (WOMAN) THAT WAS SENT FROM ABOVE?

O MAN, ARE YOU BLESSED WITH "THE PROOF OF GOD'S HOLY LOVE"?

COMPOSED JANUARY 16, 2011 AROUND 2:00 PM.

OTHER PUBLISHED BOOKS BY: BARBARA ANN MARY MACK

THE PRESENT TESTAMENT VOLUME TWO

BOOK 1: YOU ARE HOLY GROUNDS
BOOK 2: DIVINE EXCITEMENT
BOOK 3: HERE COMES THE BRIDE
BOOK 4: YOURS
BOOK 5: THE GREATEST STORY EVER TOLD
BOOK 6: FORBIDDEN LOVE
BOOK 7: THE POWER OF DIVINE LOVE
BOOK 8: LET THE CELEBRATION BEGIN
BOOK 9: YOU REPRESENT US, SAYS THE LORD!
BOOK 10: WE DID IT (LET US REJOICE)!
BOOK 11: THERE IS PEACE IN THE VALLEY OF LOVE TODAY
BOOK 12: THROUGH THE DOOR (THE LORD JESUS)
BOOK 13: WELCOME! YOU MAY ENTER
BOOK 14: SWEET CALVARY (I SEE YOU)
BOOK 15: THE NAILS: THE SWEET, SWEET, NAILS
BOOK 16: THE SOUND OF THE WHIPS
BOOK 17: COMFORTED BY THE WOUNDS OF CHRIST JESUS (THE SEQUEL)
BOOK 18: I HAVE WEPT WITH THE FAMILIES AND FRIENDS OF THE SLAIN ONES
BOOK 19: MY EXTENSION (BARBARA) OF HOLY LOVE
BOOK 20: IN THE REALM OF PLENTY
BOOK 21: MY GOD: THEY DO NOT KNOW (TEACH THEM, MY DAUGHTER)
BOOK 22: THE REALM OF ANIMATION HAS ENTERED EARTH
BOOK 23: WHAT DID WE DO IN THE LAND OF THE LIVING?
BOOK 24: THE HOLY INVITATION
BOOK 25: THY WILL BE DONE, O LORD!
BOOK 26: THE DIVINE PROMISE
BOOK 27: HOLY PASSION (GOD'S DIVINE EXPRESSIONS)
BOOK 28: YOU'RE (ALMIGHTY GOD) MY EVERYTHING!
BOOK 29: ALL MINE!
BOOK 30: THE RESURRECTION
BOOK 31: TEACH US YOUR WISDOM, DEAR LORD!

THE PRESENT TESTAMENT VOLUME THREE

BOOK 1. BARBARA: THE SECOND PRODIGY
BOOK 2. I AM THE GREAT AND HOLY ORCHESTRATOR OF LIFE, SAYS THE LORD!
BOOK 3. ROYALTY (THE HOLY TRINITY) HAS ENTERED EARTH!
BOOK 4. FOOD FROM HEAVEN'S THRONE OF LOVE
BOOK 5. THE ARRANGEMENT
BOOK 6. I SALUTE YOU, O LORD!
BOOK 7. IN THE MIDST OF THE PIT
BOOK 8. NO MORE TEARS, MY BROTHER
BOOK 9. THERE IS NO END: I AM OMEGA!
BOOK 10. I BREATHED YOU INTO EXISTENCE
BOOK 11. YOUR OMNIPRESENCE MAKES ME WEEP, DEAR LORD!
BOOK 12. THE EPIPHANY
BOOK 13. THEY BELIEVE, MY LORD, IN YOU
BOOK 14. I HAVE WITNESSED THE BIRTHS AND DEATHS OF YOUR CHILDREN:
OUR CHILDREN
BOOK 15. FOLLOW MY VOICE ALONE, SAYS THE LORD!
BOOK 16. THE ROYAL ONES
BOOK 17. A CALL TO HOLINESS
BOOK 18. SWEET PERFUME (ALMIGHTY GOD) FROM HEAVEN
BOOK 19. THE GREAT AND HOLY RECONCILIATION
BOOK 20. THE GIFT OF A FAITHFUL AND OBEDIENT COUPLE
BOOK 21. THE ENTRANCE TO LOVE
BOOK 22. A BIRTHDAY WISH
BOOK 23. THE GREATEST STORY EVER TOLD!
BOOK 24. GO, AND TELL IT ON THE MOUNTAIN!
BOOK 25. A MESSAGE OF LOVE FROM HASHEM (GD)